Finding the Wind Beneath Our Wings

By Colquitt Nash

Published by
Spiritbuilding Publishers
9700 Ferry Road, Waynesville, Ohio 45068

FINDING THE WIND BENEATH OUR WINGS
By Colquitt Nash

ISBN: 978–1–955285–73–5

Spiritbuilding
PUBLISHERS

spiritbuilding.com

Table of Contents

Introduction

You may have heard that an eagle ahead of an oncoming storm from a high perch will wait until the last minute and then jump from its perch into the storm using the strong winds to carry it above the storm. As exciting as that is to imagine, it is not entirely true. It is true eagles use the wind, even strong winds, as an updraft to help them gain altitude. The higher they can climb on an updraft the easier it is for them to soar over great distances.

In thinking about wind beneath the wings of an eagle, we should also remember from our days in elementary school science class that wind under the wing of an airplane is critical for lifting the aircraft into the air and keeping it aloft. We were taught the air moving over the top of the wing, because of its increased speed going over the curved portion of the upper side of the wing, created lower air pressure allowing the higher air pressure under the wing to push it upward thus causing "lift". That is basically correct with a minor tweak. The speed of the air moving over the top of the wing creates lower pressure. Because the air under the wing moves slower, there is more air pressure. The difference between those pressures and the air striking the front of the wing and deflected downward results in a force that lifts the plane and its contents to its desired altitude. It takes not only the air or wind but also the wing itself, specifically the angle and shape of the wing.

Sometimes I fear we are looking for something else to do the work for us when our lives need a higher altitude. We want to be passive recipients of a power that will lift us above our problems and carry us to a better place. There is such a power and hope. However, that "wind" must be accompanied by the angle or shape of our lives working in tandem with it.

There are those who talk about needing a spiritual healing, a renewing of their lives, something to restore joy, meaning and purpose. If that describes you, there is hope. You may not find yourself soaring immediately, but as you trim your wings to meet the oncoming wind and find the right shape and angle of your life, you will soar.

The promise of Scripture is true, "Though youths grow weary and tired, and vigorous young men stumble badly, yet those who wait for the Lord will gain new strength; they will mount up with wings like eagles, they will run and not get tired, they will walk and not become weary." (Isaiah 40:30–31)

May God bless you as you find His wind beneath your wings.

Lesson 1

What Are We Talking About?

In our culture, the word *spirituality* has many and varied meanings. The adjective *spiritual* also carries a diversity of ideas which can sometimes cause misunderstandings between people using the word to describe the object of their discussion.

For instance, spiritual healing is:

1. The third album by the death-metal band Death, released in February 1990. The title comes from the era when faith healer Peter Popoff was exposed as a fraud by James Randi on The Tonight Show starring Johnny Carson. This album is currently out of print.

2. A form of alternative medicine in which spirits, normally of the dead, assist in curing the afflicted.

3. The use of spiritual means in treating disease.

Spiritual healing can also refer to the self-empowerment or self-actualization process or steps within those processes which often occur with individuals seeking enlightenment or meaning in their lives. So, which one might best fit this discussion?

I believe we first must agree on a basic supposition for this discussion. That supposition is that each human being is a three-faceted being—body, mind, and soul.

A basic premise of our Christian faith is that God is a three-faceted being— God (sometimes known as the Father), Jesus (known as Christ or Son) and the Holy Spirit. Whether we call this the Trinity or the Godhead, we are talking about the same thing. We see this concept revealed in passages such as Matthew 28:19 where Jesus says we are to make disciples by baptizing them 'in the name of the Father and of the Son and of the Holy Spirit.' Paul also describes this three-faceted nature in 2 Corinthians 13:14 when he prays that, 'the grace of the Lord Jesus Christ, and the love of God, and the fellowship of the Holy Spirit' be with the Corinthian Christians. This concept began at the very beginning as Genesis 1:26 records God saying, 'Let us make man in Our image.'

If we are created in the image of a three-faceted being, it stands to reason that we also have three facets to our nature. By inspiration, Paul shares that concept with the Christians at Thessalonica when he wrote in 1 Thessalonians 5:23, 'Now may the God of peace Himself sanctify you entirely; and may your spirit and soul and body be preserved complete...' The writer of Hebrews seems to share this same idea when he writes in Hebrews 4:12 that the word of God is 'active and sharper than any two-edged sword, and piercing as far as the division of soul and spirit, or both joints and marrow, and able to judge the thoughts and intentions of the heart.'

Taking the wording of 1 Thessalonians 5:23, perhaps we might illustrate this idea in the following chart.

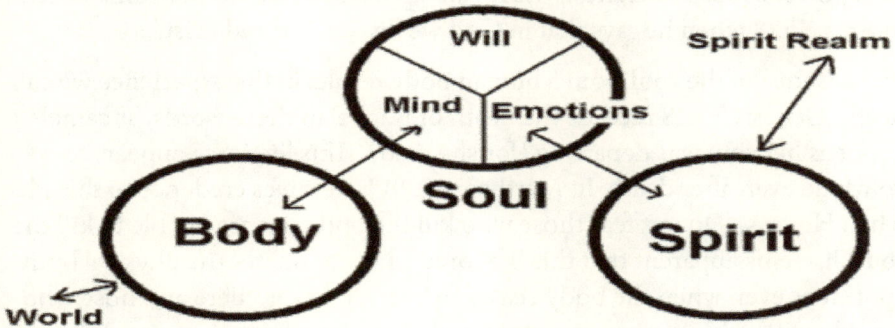

We generally do not have any problem understanding the bodily part of our make-up. We easily recognize the physical parts that form our human bodies. The body is what makes direct contact with the physical world around us through our senses—sight, smell, hearing, touch, and taste. We may begin to have a little more difficulty when we look at soul.

In Hebrew, the word for soul is *nephesh* which basically means *breath*.[1] This word is generally used to identify the immaterial, animating force within something giving that object what we call *life* as seen in Genesis 2:7 when 'the Lord God formed man of dust from the ground and breathed into his nostrils the breath of life; and man became a living being.' It is a word referring to conscious existence—able to interact with one's environment and aware of its own existence.

It appears that this life force is shared by human beings and animals alike. Ecclesiastes 3:19 says 'the fate of the sons of men and fate of beasts is the same. As one dies so dies the other; indeed, they all have the same breath.' It is interesting to note that in the account of creation in the book of Genesis, that the word *nephesh* is only used of human beings and the animal kingdom including fish, fowl, and other creatures. The word is not found when describing the plants—trees, grass, herbs, etc.

Although plants are considered *alive*, deriving nourishment from the elements of the earth, they are never called souls. Plants have life as well as animals, however, a plant's interaction with its environment does not bring about any conscious awareness of itself. Granted, some plants do react to stimuli, such as a Venus flytrap, but not in any conscious way as a human being or animal reacts to the stimuli around them.

Some have also noted that the distinction made in Genesis between plants and the soul of animals and human beings lies in the fact that those creations described as having souls are able to move from place to place under their own power as seen in Genesis 1:21. Paul appears to refer to this same criteria in Acts 17:28 when he says that in God we 'live, move and exist.'

The absence of the soul from a human body results in the experience we call death. Genesis 35:18 records the death of Rachel in these words, 'it came about as her soul was departing (for she died).' This life force appears to continue even after death. In Matthew 10:28 Jesus gives credence to this idea when He says, 'Do not fear those who kill the body but are unable to kill the soul.' It seems apparent that this life force which animates the physical body continues even when the body ceases to live. However, there are those who would say that Jesus' next statement in that verse proves otherwise. Jesus said in Matthew 22:32, 'I am the God of Abraham, and the God of Isaac, and the God of Jacob…He is not the God of the dead but of the living.' Surely this would point to an existence of human beings beyond death. These Old Testament characters are spoken of as still existing, although physically dead for centuries. Even in Revelation 20, where the lake of fire is spoken of as the 'second death' (v. 14), those entering there will be tormented day and night for ever and ever. (v. 10, 15) Being tormented can only happen to beings who are able to experience sensation.

The soul appears to include the mind (thoughts), will (decisions/behaviors), emotions and desires of a person. For instance, Genesis 34:8 says, "But Hamor spoke with them saying, 'The soul of my son Shechem longs for your daughter …'" Also, 1 Peter 2:11 warns us to abstain from fleshly lusts which "wage war against the soul."

Some folks call the soul the *personality* of an individual. If the soul does include a person's thoughts, decisions and behaviors, it has a direct connection to the physical body and thus can be influenced by it or can itself exert some control over the body. The natural man of 1 Corinthians 2:14 is described by a form of the word *psuche*[2] which indicates that Satan may do most of his work in this part of a person's life.

Turning our attention to the word *spirit* brings us to an area that may not be quite so clear as the former two. The Hebrew word for spirit is *ruwach*[3] which can also be translated wind or breath, but also has to do with a spirit being (good or bad). The Greek word is *pnuema*[4] again meaning breath or wind but also translated as spirit, especially used for the Holy Spirit.

In some ways, soul and spirit seem interchangeable. James 2:26 says, "for just as the body without the spirit is dead …" Here, a form of the word *pnuema* is used instead of *psuche*. However, it also seems clear in Scripture that the spirit is far more than breath, life force or emotional feeling alone. Romans 8:16 says, 'the Spirit Himself testifies with our spirit that we are children of God.' If our spirit is only breath, how could God's Holy Spirit (a functioning personality) testify to our spirit as if it had understanding and personality?

It appears that this part of a person (the spirit) is connected to God in some way we cannot fully know. This immaterial part of a person gives one the ability to have an intimate relationship with God who is 'spirit.' (John 4:24) It is that part of us to which God's Spirit appeals and teaches, that which can be transformed, and which changes us into what God would have us to be. It is also a part that we can choose to ignore. (1 Corinthians 2:11–14; Romans 12:1–2; 1 Thessalonians 5:19) Although each person has this capacity for spirit, the Bible only refers to believing Christians as being spiritually alive. (John 6:63; Romans 8:6; 2 Corinthians 3:6)

Some people might call the spirit the mind—that which is our innermost part and capable of all rational choice and thought. It does not appear that this part of a person can be reached directly by the senses of the physical body, but as the physical body has a connection with the soul perhaps, through the conscience, it may be blocked by the fleshly nature.

Going back to our question of defining spiritual healing, consider the following:

1. God created everything good and in harmony with Him. (Genesis 1:31)

2. Harmony with God (including physical health) is accomplished by following His guidelines. Disobedience to His statutes results in problems. (Exodus 15:26; Deuteronomy 28:1–2, 15)

3. God has given us what we need to know His will through His word, the Bible. It is through that word His Spirit speaks to our spirits in teaching us His commandments. (2 Peter 1:2–3; 2 Timothy 3:16–17; John 6:63)

Therefore, spiritual healing, in this study, refers to the healing of emotional distresses (guilt, etc.) brought on by ignoring or violating God's statutes for our lives which leads to inappropriate choices or reactions by helping us to open our spirits to the teaching of God's Spirit and by choosing to align our soul (decisions and behaviors) with God's teaching to relieve the spiritual tension we find affecting our emotions and our lives.

QUESTIONS

1. What are your key takeaways from these thoughts?

2. Do you agree/disagree with the statement that human beings have three facets or parts to them? Why or why not?

3. How would you define spirituality?

4. What is your reaction to the final paragraph of this lesson? How would you define spiritual healing?

Lesson 2

The Struggle to Change

Carl Sandburg is reported to have once said, "There is an eagle in me that wants to soar, and there is a hippopotamus in me that wants to wallow in the mud."[5]

An illustration of that might be a man pulled over by police officer. "Sir, I clocked you doing 85 in a 55 mile-an-hour zone," the policeman said as he approached the car. The driver said, "My cruise control was set on 60, perhaps you should recalibrate your instrument." The driver's wife riding next to him said, "Now dear, you know this car doesn't have a cruise control on it." "Can't you keep your mouth shut?" retorted the driver. His wife continued, "You should be glad your radar detector went off when it did." The officer began to make out a 2nd ticket for illegal detector. Again, the man said, "Why don't you be quiet?" The officer then said, "I notice you're not wearing your seatbelt." Replying to the officer the driver said, "I undid it to get to my wallet." His wife calmly said, "Dear, you know you never wear a seatbelt." As officer wrote 3rd ticket, the driver gruffly said, "Why don't you just shut up?" Unable to restrain himself, the officer asked, "Ma'am, does your husband always speak to you like this?" "Oh no, officer, only when he's been drinking," was her quick reply.

I think there is a part of us all that wants to fly like an eagle, but we get too accustomed to wallowing in the mud. We all have our dreams and visions; yet as we get older, life's realities convince us to settle for less—or to forget our dreams altogether. We get the message, "This is just the way the system works," and eventually we get sucked into the system while our dreams fade away.

For any healing to take place, whether physical or spiritual, one key question must be answered by the one who is affected. It is the question Jesus asked a lame man in John 5:6, "Do you wish to get well?"

We recognize the story of the lame man at the pool of Bethesda. John's gospel relates this pool was by the Sheep Gate in Jerusalem. This gate was on the northeastern portion of the wall facing across the Kidron Valley toward the Mount of Olives. The pool located inside the gate was north of the Temple and surrounded by five porticoes or covered colonnades. Long disputed in archeological circles, its location was discovered in the 19th century and confirmed by digs as late as 1964.

The significance of this pool lay in the belief that an angel would descend and stir the waters. Following that stirring, it was held the first person into the pool would be healed of their infirmity. Thus, John records in John 5:3 a multitude of blind, lame and folks with withered limbs congregated in the area and waited.

The man in which we are interested, according to John, had been ill for thirty–eight years. We are not told how long he had been coming to the pool. We can only assume it had been quite a while. It is to this man that Jesus walks and asks him the question. The man probably looked at Jesus with an expression that said, "Isn't it obvious that's why I am here?" However, the only words John records him speaking are words offering excuses for why he wasn't healed. His basic response was to blame others. His response sounds all too familiar, doesn't it?

Quite a few people say they want to overcome their problems but are not prepared to do their part to make it happen. Many psychologists will say that people don't really want to be cured. What they want is relief; a cure is too painful. One surgeon said that many of his patients who come to him would rather he operate on their body than operate on their lifestyle and that only about 25% of his patients accept responsibility for their wellness.

It seems to boil down to the fact that we don't want to change from that which we are accustomed. However, change and growth are a part of life. One illustration of this comes from Gail Sheehy as she wrote:

> In my book *Passages* I used the analogy of the lobster, which grows
> by developing and shedding a series of hard, protective shells. Each
> time it expands from within, the confining shell must be sloughed
> off, and it is left unprotected until a new covering grows. We, too, in
> each passage from one stage of human growth to the next, mut shed
> a protective structure. We, too, are left exposed and vulnerable—
> but also yeasty and embryonic again. At such points we enjoy a
> *heightened potential* for making a real stretch of growth. But we can
> also fall back, lose ground, give up, or simply ignore the impulse to

change and remain stuck in our shells. Whatever we do, the future will be rendered better or worse but, in any case, restructured.[6]

One of the things making us uniquely human is the ability to choose change. We are not simply beings who react to the stimuli around us (as behavioral psychologists would assert). We can think beyond the stimulus and choose our response. If we really do want to soar, why is it we find it so difficult to get off the ground to change? May I suggest, from experience and observation, some of those reasons?

Perhaps one reason is because of our perspective. We can see things in other people we do not see so easily in ourselves. We may understand we need to change; we simply cannot see what it is that should be changed. Just as we can see things that need changed in others, it may be others can help us see things within ourselves. One inherent problem in having others give us feedback is that in hearing that feedback one or more of our *hot buttons* may be pushed.

Another problem with perspective is that, as we become aware of things we need to change, we may believe what we have been or been doing has been wrong or not good enough. We sometimes learn something new and then apply this new knowledge to the past to prove we were bad because we did not know what we do now. Before going on, can we take a reality check? We cannot know what we do not know before we learn it. We should always be in the process of learning new things. What is important is moving forward from that point, using that information, and not using it as a stick to beat ourselves up for the past.

Another reason for not changing may be related to our programming. That is not to say we are machines. However, many of our emotional and behavioral habits are formed in early childhood. We simply spend many of the subsequent years practicing those things. This does not mean we *cannot* change, we *can*. In fact, I believe most of us were more persistent as children in trying to change the way we did things, than we are now as adults. If as a child we had the same persistence about changing as we apparently do now, how many of us would have learned to walk, ride a bicycle or any number of other activities we now do? Change is possible.

For others, the obstacle to change is the payoff. That is, staying the same has more value to us than changing. Some feel they have more invested in holding the status quo than in changing and moving forward. There are those out there who would boil this thought down to pain and pleasure. We only change when the pain being experienced is greater than the pleasure to be gained. For instance, I may know I need to lose weight, but the idea of eating cupcakes on the couch is more appealing that exercising. In this case, the pleasure I am experiencing is greater than the pain of working out. Sometimes that balance is affected by a health crisis or a stern warning from a doctor. At times our inability to change may also be affected by the pain or pleasure of those around us and how they would have to change.

The story is told of a man who was told by his doctor, "You have got to change. Ask your wife to fix you more nutritious meals; stop working like a dog; you and your wife make a budget and stick to it and ask your kids to give you some time to relax. If you don't, you could be dead in a month." The man replied, "Would you tell my wife that? It would sound more official coming from you." The doctor agreed and the man brought his wife into the room and returned to the waiting area for her to return. Shortly she came out, hugged her husband, and said, "I talked to your doctor, and he said you only have 30 days to live."

I am convinced that the greatest hurdle to overcome is fear. It is said there are only two innate fears within human beings. All other fears are *learned*. Those two fears are loud noises and falling.[7] What do we fear about change?

The obvious thing we fear is the unknown. We are already familiar with how things are now. We have become accustomed to them. However, we are not sure how things might be if we change—even if those changes have been things we have dreamed of for years. Or it may be our fear of being rejected. Those around us are accustomed to how we are and if we change, they may have to change the way they relate to us. We fear they may not want to remain in our circle, and we would be alone.

I believe we also fear loss—in this case the loss of life, death. It is not that we believe any changes would result in our death, we simply fear death. Many perceive death as losing all they know, the physical sensations of joy, fulfillment, etc. Those whose lives are full and robust then lose a great deal when they die. Therefore, some folks draw their circles of life very small so that when they do die, they have not lost very much. Hebrews 2:14–15 says,

> Therefore, since the children share in flesh and blood, He Himself likewise also partook of the same, that through death He might render him powerless who had the power of death, that is, the devil, and might free those who through fear of death were subject to slavery all their lives.

Satan has convinced many that this is all there is and since they fear leaving it behind, they restrict what they do and the full enjoyment of life.

Remember, however, our question, "Do you wish to get well?" Answering that question in the affirmative is a positive step in the right direction in finding the wind beneath our wings.

One key principle to remember in bringing about change is to have a reason for change. We might also add having an urgency to change, not an urgency because of impending doom but an urgency of achieving a dream. Plainly stated, a person must want to change more than they want to remain as they are.

On May 20, 1873, U.S. Patent #139,121 was issued to Levi Strauss and Jacob Davis for their denim "waist overalls" (jeans).[8] Strauss had proposed the use of the denim cloth and Davis had proposed copper rivets to make the pressure points stronger. The problem was that sitting close to a campfire, a person regularly got a case of Hot Rivet Syndrome. This persisted until 1933 when Walter Hass, Sr., the president of Levi Strauss went on a camping trip and fell prey to Hot Rivet Syndrome. Finding out that nearly every other man in the group had experienced the same thing, Hass went into the next board meeting and the rivet in the crotch area was eliminated. The moral to learn from this story is that some people change when they see the light, and some only change when they feel the heat. Which one will you be?

Another key principle is the confident belief that change is possible. As a child I remember my mother taking my sister and me to watch a circus setting up at the edge of the town where we lived. I marveled at how the elephants were kept in their places by a small rope tied to a large peg hammered into the ground. Later I learned how that was possible. As you may know, a young elephant is captured, and a heavy chain is placed around its leg and attached to a metal ring cemented into a piling in the ground. The young elephant struggles long and hard to pull itself free, but it cannot. Eventually it resigns itself to the fact that if a rope or chain is attached to its leg and to something in the ground it cannot pull free. How powerful belief is—for good or bad.

We may tell ourselves, and anyone else who will listen, "I can't change. This is just the way I am." Several folks have been credited with the statement, Warren Buffet is credited with the statement "The chains of habit are too light to be felt until they are to heavy to be broken."[9] Indeed, our habits do have power, but not ultimate and infinite power. Our habits do have a way of catching up with us, however. Do you remember the story of Samson in Judges 13–16, especially chapter 16? Samson was a man blessed by God with strength when it was needed. Yet Samson let some of his habits, like romancing foreign women, cause him problems. After teasing Delilah twice, he finally revealed the source of his strength which was his hair. We know the rest of the story. Delilah had it cut and when the Philistines came again, Samson was captured. Judges 16:21 records that Samson was blinded and chained to a grinder in the prison, pushing a great stone around in circles to crush the grain into flour. So, too, our habits can blind us to what we have become and chain us into going in circles.

The light at the end of this tunnel for us is found in the truth of God's word. Jeremiah 29:1 says, "For I know the plans I have for you, declares the Lord, plans for welfare and not for calamity to give you a future and a hope." When we, like David, feel trapped in the despair of what we have done, remember his words of Psalm 51:10–14,

Create in me a clean heart, O God, and renew a steadfast spirit within me. Do not cast me away from your presence and do not take your Holy Spirit from me. Restore to me the joy of your salvation and sustain me with a willing spirit. Then I will teach transgressors your ways, and sinners will be converted to you. Deliver me from blood guiltiness, O God, the God of my salvation; then my tongue will joyfully sing of your righteousness.

Peter reminds us in Acts 3:19, "Therefore repent and return so that your sins may be wiped away, in order that times of refreshing may come from the presence of the Lord."

These verses are not presented to say that where we are is sin, but that change is possible and a change that brings fullness and joy. This change is possible through a belief and trust in God and a trusting obedience to His leading and will. The wiseman of Proverbs 3:5–8 says,

Trust in the Lord with all your heart and do not lean on your own understanding. In all your ways acknowledge him and he will make your paths straight. Do not be wise in your own eyes, fear the Lord and turn away from evil. It will be healing to your body and refreshment to your bones.

However, belief or urgency is meaningless unless acted upon. Ecclesiastes 9:10 encourages us that, "whatever your hand finds to do, do it with all your might."

Change for the better is good and necessary. Change is life. The only question is whether the changes we make will be *proactive* or *reactive*. We can create any number of excuses for not changing. Life goes by fast without regard to our excuses. In a month, a week, or a year, will your life be different? Will the things holding you back still be holding you back? At some point in the future when you look back at your life will you wonder how you got to where you are, or will you see the steps that you took to get you where you are? As Professor Irwin Corey, a Vaudeville comic and actor used to say, "If you don't change direction soon, you'll end up where you are going."

QUESTIONS

1. What are your key takeaways from these thoughts?

2. What hot buttons do you have and why do certain things cause such a reaction from and within you? It is important for us to know this.

3. Which reason(s) might you have for not choosing to change?

4. Often, when people analyze where they are in life, they are discouraged. However, where you are is where you are and that's okay. The important question is "Where do I want to be and what do I need to get there?" How would you respond to that question?

5. Do you wish to get well?

Lesson 3

Misbeliefs

"Why do I feel the way I do?" we cry. The typical response is to blame something or someone else. "It's my wife/husband/children's fault because they...." "I don't like my job." Some blame their church because the preacher is/isn't _____; the people aren't friendly; etc.

There is generally at least one thing in each of our lives we would like to change. It may be difficult to change the circumstances, but there is one thing we can change that will lead to healing the hurts we seem to have. The interesting thing is that the problem and the solution are the very same thing. Solomon said in Proverbs 23:7, "As a man thinks within himself so he is...."

Contrary to popular belief, it is not the circumstances or events either past or present that make us feel the way we do; it is our interpretation of those circumstances and events. Our feelings are caused by what we continually tell ourselves whether verbally or mentally.

Years ago, a poll was taken of about 5,000 middle–class men and women, single and married. It was determined that the happiness level of each group was almost even. What was interesting was that those who were married envied those who were single. Their belief was that single people are happy because they can do whatever they want whenever they desire since they are responsible only for themselves. Those who were single, however, envied those who were married. The reason for this was that those who were single felt since the married couples had someone special to share life with and a family their happiness level should be higher.

The story is told of a wise man sitting at the city gate being approached by a traveler. The traveler asked, "What kind of people live in this city?" The wise man responded, "What kind of people live in the city from which you come?" "They are self-centered, stingy and unfriendly," the traveler said. He was told, "You will find the same kind here." The traveler moved on. Another traveler approached the wise man and asked the same question. When asked what kind of people lived in the city from which he came, the traveler said,

"They are good, kind and loving people." The wise man smiled and said, "You will find the same kind of people here." The answer was correct for each traveler because the difference was in what each traveler thought.

The key principle comes down to what we tell ourselves through our thoughts is true because the way we act, feel and live is based upon what we believe. Our beliefs in turn come from what some term as self–talk, the messages we tell ourselves. The problem is that much of what we tell ourselves may not be true. Rather than being true beliefs they are misbeliefs. A misbelief is generally something that appears to be true but is not; these misbeliefs are often the cause of our destructive behavior. Let's look at some of the key misbeliefs keeping the wind from beneath our wings.

Some folks believe that to be happy they must get what they want. This leads to some thoughts such as: my wants are the most important ones in the world, and it is terrible if I don't get what I want and unfair if someone has it when I don't. They begin to believe they will only be happy if they get what they want. Some Christians may even believe God's only desire is for His children to be happy. If they are not getting what they want, then either there is something wrong with them as a Christian or God does not hear or answer their prayers.

The truth of the matter is, it may be inconvenient or uncomfortable not to have something, but it is not the end of life as we know it. It is not a terrible thing not to have every need met on our terms or our schedule. Jesus said in Luke 12:23, "Life is more than food." To a man who probably held this misbelief Jesus said in Luke 12:15, "Even when one has an abundance does his life consist of his possessions." We need to tell ourselves and believe the truth of Matthew 6:33, "Seek first His kingdom and His righteousness and all these things will be added to you." Paul reminded the Philippian Christians that God would supply all their needs according to his riches in glory in Christ Jesus. (Philippians 4:19) Notice the word *needs* and do not replace it with the word *wants*.

Many may believe it is terrible to have hurt feelings. Believing this, they tell themselves they must avoid people and situations that may hurt their feelings. This belief carries the corollary belief that they must make everyone happy. Compound this idea with the attitude that a Christian should never feel hurt, and that mixture becomes a heavy burden to carry.

It is not unspiritual to have hurt feelings. God has created us as beings who have feelings—a whole range of them. At times we will feel hurt or slighted, but those feelings do not define our spirituality. If we feel we must protect ourselves, let us tell ourselves to stand behind the shield of God Himself. God promised Abraham in Genesis 15:1 that He would be a shield to him. Read the Psalms and see how David must have felt hurt and slighted but kept running to God as a refuge. (Psalm 16:1; 25:19–20; 61:1–4; etc.)

A close relative of the previous misbelief is the one that says: to be happy I must be loved by everyone. We tell ourselves we must do whatever it takes to make people like us. We convince ourselves that those who are not loved are failures; therefore if no one likes us we are failures. This belief keeps us running rapidly from one place to another, changing colors quicker than a chameleon as we must be whatever the person we are with desires. This effectively leaves us with no identity since we are what others want us to be.

To stop this merry–go–round we need to speak, hear, and believe the simple truth that we are loved unconditionally by God. Do you remember one of your first memory verses from Bible class as a child? "God so loved the world" (John 3:16) Someone has suggested that to help us move from a global vision we need to replace *our name* where the word *world* is. Like the sun shining on a lake covers the whole surface it appears as a single ray directly to us as we stand on the shoreline, so God's love covering the whole world is also a direct connection to us.

On top of that, Jesus loves us. Years ago, Karl Barth, a renowned theologian of the 20th century, spoke to the students of the University of Chicago. During a question–and–answer period, a student asked, "Dr. Barth, could you summarize your life's work of theology in one sentence?" Pausing for just a moment, Dr. Barth looked at the student and replied, "Yes I can in the words of a song I learned at my mother's knee: Jesus loves me, this I know, for the Bible tells me so."[10]

I can only imagine how many people are telling themselves that to be happy things must go right and be right for them. Generally, I believe we define being right by using our own yardstick. Therefore, we must defend everything we do or think because there is no room for mistakes, and we *must* be right. If we are not right or correct or if we make a mistake, we tell ourselves we are inept.

Surely you have made mistakes. I have and the sun still came up the next morning in the east. The truth related to mistakes is in learning from them and doing things differently the next time. They say insanity is doing the same thing and expecting different results. However, if I must be right, then I may not try another way. Another lesson about mistakes is to learn the lesson of forgiving myself as God forgives. We may not be able to forget, but we can begin fresh. We are where we are and that's okay. The key question is, "Where do we go from here?

Many folks who call themselves Christian may believe they must always be happy and act happy despite the hardship or trouble in which they find themselves. They believe that feeling unhappy or upset is an indication of not being a good Christian and it would be a terrible thing for people to believe that about them, or for themselves to believe that. Therefore, they hide their real feelings and paste a big smile on their face.

It is true that James tells us to count it all joy when we encounter trials. (James 1:2) Paul also exhorted the Philippian Christians to rejoice always. (Philippians 4:8) It is also true that there are times when we feel overwhelmed. Didn't Paul also write about being afflicted in every way, crushed, perplexed, persecuted, and struck down? (2 Corinthians 4:8–9) However, don't skip over the other words in that last passage. Paul says that although bad things may happen to us, they do not crush us, cause us to despair or destroy us. I sometimes think we stop reading too soon in 1 Corinthians 10:13. We understand we are in the same way as other people; the difference is that God has promised, and is providing, His strength to help us through.

It was the philosopher Friedrich Nietzsche who said, "What does not destroy me makes me stronger."[11] Life will test us, sometimes to what seems to be the breaking point. Upon completing the test, there is a reward. It was God who said in Romans 5:3–5,

> Exult in … tribulations knowing that tribulation brings about perseverance; and perseverance proven character; and proven character hope; and hope does not disappoint, because the love of God has been poured out within our hearts through the Holy Spirit who was given to us.

It is not only God who helps us through our struggles, but also our Christian brothers and sisters. Galatians 6:2 says, "Bear one another's burdens and so fulfill the law of Christ." Some may point to verse 5 of that context and say, 'Paul also says I need to carry my own load,[12] and that doesn't leave much for helping others.' The word in verse 5 is a word that is a diminutive of a word meaning a load. The connotation is that of a backpack versus a bundle of firewood. The word in verse 2 is a different word meaning an excessive load or burden that can easily take away a person's ability to carry it.[13] The call is not to take away another's burden, but to help them when they are overwhelmed. We should encourage one another and hold each other up so that together we may cross the line together as some of the runners did at a 1976 Special Olympics race in Spokane, Washington.

Although we may not see them quickly, we can become aware of the misbeliefs we hold. The harder part of the equation is overcoming those misbeliefs—and they can be overcome. The first hurdle to clear, however, is one more misbelief.

Some Christians feel that a Christian should not change an unpleasant situation even if they could do so. It seems their rationale comes from Paul's statement to the Corinthian Christians in 1 Corinthians 7:20 when he said, "Each man must remain in that condition in which he was called." Again, let me encourage you not to stop reading too soon. Continuing that context through verse 21, Paul says, "Were you called while a slave? Do not worry about it; but if you are able to become free, rather do that." Paul certainly encouraged slaves, but he also says, through inspiration, that should an opportunity present itself to change that situation, by all means do it. Christians do not have to simply *muddle through* difficult circumstances or miss out on the fullness and joy of life if there is a way to do that. There is a way to find the wind beneath your wings and soar.

Simply stated, the steps to overcoming the misbeliefs in your mind are:

1. Identify the misbelief.

2. Remove the misbelief by challenging it with the truth of God's word.

3. Replace the misbelief by changing your thought processes and the things you tell yourself about yourself and what is happening to you.

Here is a quick test. Which of the statements below do you most hear yourself saying?

*   I am not too smart. / *Thank you, Lord, for giving me intelligence.*

*   I am unattractive. / *Thank you, Lord, for making me attractive.*

*   I can't _____ . / *Thank you, Lord, for making me able to* _____ .

*   Others are happier than me. / *Thank you, Lord, for the happiness in my life.*

*   People don't like me. / *Thank you, Lord, for making me likable.*

*   I have no talents. / *Thank you, Lord, for the talents you have given me.*

*   I am lonely. / *Thank you, Lord, for being my faithful and closest companion.*

When seen like this, it is easy to identify the misbeliefs we may hold. Removing the misbelief is a little harder. It is done, however, by arguing against and challenging the misbelief on the left with the truth on the right and letting that truth replace the misbelief. For instance, if I were to tell you not to think about baby pandas for the next minute, could you do it? You could if you made the decision to think about pink elephants instead.

Historically we have seen how this has happened to people. For many years people "believed" the mark of Cain (Genesis 4:15) was black skin. This was even preached in churches adding that such a mark showed God's displeasure and that the other punishment of that context meant such a person was inferior. It was only a short step to believing that such people were only good for slave labor. It has taken centuries of challenging that misbelief with the truth that people with a different skin color than yourself have the same standing in God's sight and should also be respected as worthwhile individuals in society.

It is by replacing the misbeliefs we hold with the truth that change happens in our lives. That truth should be the truth of God's Word. Jesus said in John 8:32, "you will know the truth and the truth will make you free." Paul wrote in 2 Timothy 3:16–17 that, "all Scripture is inspired by God and profitable for teaching, for reproof, for correction, for training in righteousness; that the man of God may be adequate, equipped for every good work."

God's word tells us we are made in God's image, blessed by Him, and pronounced good. (Genesis 1:26–31) We are fearfully and wonderfully made. (Psalm 139:13–14) Jesus teaches that God knows us so well that even the number of the hairs on our head is known and that God will not forget us. (Luke 12:7)

By the way, there is something interesting in that last verse. Jesus says in v. 6 that God does not forget any sparrow and that you are of more value than many sparrows. But let me ask you a question, "Have you ever felt like the fifth sparrow?" Sometimes it is easy to get lost in a crowd, especially when it appears you are not worth much.

To really understand this, we also need to read Matthew 10:29 where Jesus gives the going rate for sparrows which were items of commerce during Jesus' day as food items according to some scholars. In the passage in Matthew, Jesus says, "Are not two sparrows sold for a cent?" In Luke's account He remarks that five are sold for two cents. A little quick math reveals that two cents should have only bought four, but apparently if you bought two, one was thrown in for free making its value nothing. Yet even that worthless sparrow was not forgotten by God. Remember that promise when you feel like that fifth sparrow.

Replace the untruth that you are worthless to God by reaffirming the truth of Psalm 139:1–12 where David says you are never outside the presence or care of God. Believe God as He speaks through the prophet in Isaiah 43:1–2,

> But now says the Lord, your Creator, O Jacob, and He who formed you, O Israel, do not fear, for I have redeemed you; I have called you by name; you are Mine! When you pass through the waters, I will be with you; and through the rivers, they will not overflow you. When you walk through the fire, you will not be scorched, nor will the flame burn you.

Above all else, replace the misbelief that you don't matter to God by remembering and believing the truth of John 3:16, Romans 5:8–10 and Romans 8:31–39.

The wise man said in Proverbs 18:21, "Death and life are in the power of the tongue." That is not only true about what we say regarding others, but also ourselves. The healing we desire will be helped when we cease to harm ourselves by our misbeliefs and believe the truths of God about ourselves.

QUESTIONS

1. What are your key takeaways from these thoughts?

2. Looking back over your life, in which direction is the slope of your life's graph going? Are you moving upward, level, or descending?

3. What are some of your misbeliefs? Make a list of what they are and then find a verse in the Bible that confronts and contradicts that misbelief with the truth of God. Spend time memorizing those verses.

4. If you heard someone talking to themselves like you may sometimes talk too yourself, what would you say to them?

Lesson 4

Doubt

Doubt is a normal, human experience—even for Christians. One key aspect of doubt is to discern from where it is coming. Some people say doubt comes from Satan. Perhaps that is true, but it may also oversimplify the point. What is causing your doubts? Is it because something bad happened? Is it because you see others who believe fervently, and you don't think you are as passionate? Is it that God just seems far away from you? A person needs to examine the cause of their doubts to face them and change.

On December 31, 1965[14], Charles Schultz's Peanuts characters Charlie Brown and Lucy were having a discussion. Charlie Brown said, "Next year I'm going to be a changed person!" Lucy replied, "That's a laugh, Charlie Brown." Charlie retorted, "I mean it! I'm going to be strong and firm." Lucy walks away saying, "Forget it. You'll always be wishy-washy." Charlie Brown calls after her, "Why can't I change just a little bit? I'll be wishy one day and washy the next!"

Other people doubt us, and we begin to doubt ourselves. We use the word a lot, but what does it mean?

According to Webster, doubt means: to be uncertain in opinion or belief, to be inclined to unbelief.[15] When someone talks about a legislator's upcoming vote and says their vote is still in doubt, it does not mean that they will not vote; it simply means no one knows which way they will vote. Two friends may be talking about something that will soon happen and one says, "No doubt". That statement generally means there is a high probability of that thing happening. But when a lawyer speaks of something being beyond the shadow of a doubt, he is talking about a certainty. So, what is it?

In the Greek, the word generally translated doubt is διακρίνω (diakrinō) made up of two words meaning to separate through.[16] It carries the idea of having two minds and wavering between two points. Elijah asked the people of Israel in 1 Kings 18:21 how long they would hesitate (NASB) or waver

(NIV) before deciding once and for all whether Baal or Jehovah was truly God. Doubt is basically the inability to decide which way to go or what to believe and act accordingly. In the New Testament, James says a person who doubt is double–minded and tossed about like someone on the waves of the sea. (James 1:6)

Someone has said that doubts occur when what we expect to happen *isn't* happening, or what shouldn't be happening *is* happening. Circumstances are in direct conflict with what we believe. This causes us to be confused and waver between the two, wondering which is right.[17] It may be doubt comes from our misbeliefs about what we can and cannot do or whether we are allowed to make mistakes and not be considered a failure.

Before going on, let's settle an intriguing question, "Is doubt the same as unbelief?" Whatever your conclusion or feeling, I believe that although they are technically not the same, they are closely related—kissing cousins you might say. The reason I believe this way is that doubt says, "I don't think that can happen." Unbelief, on the other hand, says, "No way can that happen." To illustrate what I mean, let's look at two biblical characters that lived through virtually the same experience within a few months of each other.

In Luke 1:8–18 we are introduced to a priest by the name of Zacharias who was chosen one day to be the one to enter the Holy Place of the temple to burn incense while the people prayed. Upon entering the temple, Zacharias encounters the angel Gabriel standing at the right side of the altar of incense. The angel tells Zacharias his prayers will be answered as he and his wife, Elizabeth, will have a son to be named John. Upon hearing the news, Zacharias challenges the angel's message by not only doubting the message, but basically discrediting the announcement by the fact that both he and Elizabeth were too old for this to be possible.

Pause this video clip for just a moment and analyze it. I am sure the way the announcement came certainly caught Zacharias off guard. However, if the angel's statement is correct—and we have no reason to doubt it, Zacharias had been praying for a child and should have been one to believe that God would answer prayer. Yet when the answer came, he basically said "This can't happen because we are too old." We know it could and it did, although Zacharias had to pay a price for his unbelief.

Three months later the same angel appears to a young woman named Mary and gave her the same message, "You are going to have a baby." This story from Luke 1:26–34 relates how Mary asked the angel, "How can this be since I am a virgin?" (Luke 1:34) Although the question of Zacharias and

Mary sound the same, do you hear the subtle differences? Mary wanted to know how it would happen since she apparently knew how babies arrive and she was not married, nor had been sexually active. Zacharias' question is a disguised statement of impossibility.

Questions are not the problem, even when those questions spring from doubt about how something is going to happen. Even doubt is not the problem. However, unexpressed, and unchecked doubt (having your mind closed to the explanation) grows into unbelief. Such doubt, wavering between certainty and doubt, according to James 1:6–8, engenders a spiritual instability that keeps us from receiving God's fullest blessings.

One plan to overcome doubts and doubting might include:

1. Acknowledge your doubts and fears. Some folks try to pass them off as nervousness or anxiety. Call it what it is—doubt and fear.

2. Quantify it. Ask yourself, "How much doubt and fear am I feeling on a scale of 1 to 10 (with 1 being none or very little)?" This may help you keep your feelings in perspective.

3. Imagine the worst–case scenario. How many times did your parents ask you, "What is the worst thing that could happen?" when you voiced concern over a particular situation? Then you should have practice doing this; and do not leave any details out.

4. Finally, assess the support and resources you might find to help you in coping with the worst-case scenario. In all probability, that same support and those same resources are available to you now.

Although some may say this is a negative way of looking at things, I believe that most of us generally imagine the worst by default. If that is true, then use that reflex to find strength and a reason for faith. A humorous quote attributed to many people says, "I am an old man and have known a great many troubles, but most of them never happened."[18] Realizing there are others there to help can be a great encouragement. Andrew Sinclair in his book, *Prohibition: The Era of Excess* credits Calvin Coolidge with the quote, "Never go out to meet trouble. If you will just sit still, nine cases out of ten someone will intercept it before it reaches you."[19] If that is the case, then let us also consider some other ideas.

Perhaps one of the first steps to come to your mind was to pray. After all, didn't Peter encourage us to cast all our anxiety on God because of His care for us? (1 Peter 5:7) Others may think about the prayer Jesus taught in Matthew 6:9–13. I find it interesting that verse 8 of that chapter says that

God knows what we need even before we ask. While there are those who might say that God should go ahead and give us what we need, I feel that many of us still harbor some doubt about God really knowing what we need which then carries us back to Peter's thought about casting that on God.

Bible reading and study is another good step to help us overcome doubt. Let me share this idea with you.

John the Baptist (promised son of Zacharias) was to come as the one proclaiming the coming of Jesus. He did this very confidently as John 1:29 indicates. John himself says in John 1:34 that he had seen and testified that Jesus was the Son of God. There was no doubt about it as far as he was concerned. However, life has a way of catching up with us as it did John. Herod had John imprisoned because of what he was saying about Herod's marriage. (Matthew 14:3–4) In that cell, doubts began to arise in John's mind. Matthew 11:2–6 records that John sent some of his disciples to Jesus with an important question, "Are you the Expected One, or shall we look for someone else?" Even after he had confidently told people who Jesus was, a doubt flew through his mind.

Jesus could have simply said, "Yes," or "Tell him he knows I am." Instead, he tells them to go back to John and tell him what they are seeing and hearing: the blind were receiving sight, the lame walking again, the lepers cleansed, the deaf hearing, the dead were being raised and the poor were having the good news preached to them. What would that do for John?

What you notice in most Bibles is a footnote pointing to an Old Testament prophecy of Isaiah in Isaiah 35:5–6. There the prophet said that when God would come the eyes of the blind would be opened, the ears of the deaf unstopped, the lame would leap like deer and the dumb would speak. Although Jesus did not mention the dumb speaking, He threw in lepers being healed and the dead raised. Jesus pointed John back to a promise of God as to what would happen when He (through His Son in this case) would come. In fact, verse 4 of Isaiah 35 says that these were the words to say to those with anxious hearts. Could we perhaps read that as those with doubts, like John? The gospel Jesus preached was from Isaiah 61, a favorite prophecy of the Jews about the coming of God's Messiah. Jesus told those in attendance at synagogue in Luke 4:16–21 this gospel was being fulfilled in their hearing that day.

Jesus reassured John's doubts with the word of God. Can it do the same for us? Absolutely! Just as the Bereans examined the scriptures and believed (Acts 17:11–12), the word of God can teach, correct and train us to be fully equipped to handle life. (2 Timothy 3:16–17) The catch is that we must give diligence in studying it (2 Timothy 2:15) and as Jesus said about the wise man in Matthew 7:24 not only hear but act upon that word. God's word is to be believed and trusted.

Some might think about overcoming doubt by asking for a sign from God. Isn't that what John did? Actually, several Bible characters have asked God for signs. Gideon and his fleece is perhaps the most well–remembered. Others may shudder at the thought of asking God for a sign, believing it borders on tempting or testing God. It is then pointed out that in response to Satan's temptation of Jesus to throw Himself from the temple He responded, "It is written, 'You shall not put the Lord your God to the test.'" (Luke 4:12) Let's think about this for a moment.

That quote is from Deuteronomy 6:16 where Moses tells Israel, "You shall not put the Lord your God to the test as you tested Him at Massah." As you recall, Massah was the name given a place at Rephidim after Israel had crossed the Red Sea. The Israelites were thirsty, and Moses struck the rock for water to come forth. Exodus 17:7 says this happened because the people of Israel "tested the Lord saying, 'Is the Lord among us or not?'"

The word in Hebrew is *nasah* meaning "to prove anyone, to put him to the test. Men are said to prove or tempt God by doubting, not confiding in his power or aid."[20] The Greek word is *ekparadzo* which means "to put to proof God's character and power."[21]

Notice how Israel put God to the test. They doubted He was with them. It seems inconceivable to us as we realize they had just witnessed the power of God through the plagues in Egypt. They had been protected from Pharaoh's army at the Red Sea by the pillar of fire and walked across the Red Sea on dry ground. Then, because they get thirsty, they doubt that God is with them.

It seems the problem went deeper as Numbers 14:11 reveals. God in speaking to Moses, after Israel had once more doubted God and His promise of Canaan based on the fear of the ten spies in Numbers 13, said, "How long will this people spurn Me? And how long will they not believe in Me, despite all the signs that I have performed in their midst?" This testing of God not only borders on unbelief, it is unbelief.

God again challenged His people in Malachi 3:10 by saying, "Bring the whole tithe into the storehouse so that there may be food in my house, and test me now in this, says the Lord of hosts, if I will not open up for you the widows of heaven and pour out for you a blessing until it overflows." Although not the same word used in Deuteronomy 6:16, it carries the same implications. However, this "test" seems to be more along the lines of doing what God says, so that He can prove He is faithful and will do what He has promised. Much like Leviticus 25:4–6 where God commanded the people not to sow their fields nor harvest anything from the vines in the seventh year. His promise in Leviticus 35:18–22 was that He would provide a harvest in the sixth year that would last for three years until they harvested in the eighth year. Following God's commandment and having enough food until the eight year's harvest would have been to test God and prove Him faithful in much the same way Thomas *tested* and *proved* Jesus in John 20:24–29.

Doubt can and must be changed to trust—a trust in the truth that God desires and provides for us. (Proverbs 3:5–8) Psalm 119:105 says, "Your word is a lamp unto my feet and a light to my path". It is said in the time those words were written the lamps were small. The entire path was not revealed, only the next step. We need to trust God only for the next step as we continue our journey through life.

QUESTIONS

1. What are your key takeaways from these thoughts?

2. Is doubt the same as unbelief?

3. What triggers or brings about doubt in your life?

4. Are your doubts directed toward God or yourself?

5. How do you handle doubt?

Lesson 5

A Hard Question

Wes Leonard was a cheerful, 6'4" 16-year-old athlete from Fennville, Michigan. He played football and basketball and had been called the best athlete from Fennville for the past 50 years. On the night of March 3, 2011, Wes drove the lane against Bridgman High and laid the ball in the basket with 26 seconds left in the game giving Fennville a 57–55 advantage. It proved to be the winning basket as Bridgman's last shot missed the mark. Fennville would be taking a 20–0 record into the state tournament the next week. The teams shook hands and Wes' teammates hoisted him to their shoulders then put him down for a team huddle. A few minutes later Wes Leonard collapsed to the gym floor and was rushed by ambulance to Holland Hospital about 15 minutes away. Two hours later, Wes Leonard was pronounced dead from dilated cardio myopia, an enlarged heart.

It doesn't matter whether you come from a Christian perspective or whether you approach situations like this from another spiritual vantage point, sometimes you just ask the question, "How could God let this happen?" Tragedy, whether our own or someone else's, has a way of testing our faith and calling into question most, if not all, of how we thought things were supposed to work.

From observation and experience, I believe our initial reaction to the question above is to ask additional questions. "Did God cause this?" "If God is all–powerful, why didn't He stop it?" "I was taught that God would watch over me and protect me. What happened?" "I prayed and believed, but it didn't work. Why not?" "How can I trust God after this?" "I am angry at God. Is He angry with me?"

We seem to waffle back and forth confronting God with questions and then backing off nervously so as not to antagonize Him. Is it okay to question God? The answer is, "YES!" Consider some Bible characters who did.

1. Job—"I loathe my own life; I will give full vent to my complaint; I will speak in the bitterness of my soul. I will say to God, Do not condemn me; let me know why you contend with me." (Job 10:1–2)

2. Moses—Exodus 33:12–17

3. Jonah—"Then God said to Jonah (after killing the plant), 'Do you have good reason to be angry about the plant?' And he said, 'I have good reason to be angry, even to death.'" (Jonah 4:9)

4. David—"My God, my God why have you forsaken me? Far from my deliverance are the words of my groaning. O my God, I cry by day, but you do not answer; and by night, but I have no rest." (Psalm 22:1–2)

Even God Himself says in Isaiah 41:21, "'Present your case,'" the Lord says. 'Bring forward your strong arguments,' the King of Jacob says."

God is big enough to handle the emotions and questions we give to Him. Unfortunately, our secondary reaction seems to become silent and not talk to or listen to God. If a loved one of yours believed you had done something hurtful to them and questioned your motives about it, what would you want them to do? Wouldn't you want them to talk to you? That is exactly what God want us to do. He wants us to communicate with Him:

1 Peter 5:7—"casting all your anxiety on Him, because He cares for you."

Philippians 4:6—"be anxious for nothing, but in everything by prayer and supplication with thanksgiving let your requests be made known to God."

Perhaps it is some more of our misbeliefs that get in the way of telling God how we feel. We tell ourselves that if we are good, God won't let bad things happen to us. Yet there are daily examples of bad things happening to good people. Why? Let me ask you a question. Jesus said in Matthew 7:12, "In everything, therefore, treat people the same way you want them to treat you, for this is the Law and the Prophets." True or False: If I treat someone nicely, they will treat me nicely? The realistic answer is "false." Everyone has a choice as to how they will respond to the things that happen in their life and to the people in their life.

Jesus also said in Matthew 5:45 that God causes the sun to rise on the evil and the good and sends rain on the righteous and the unrighteous. That may not be fair, but it is the way life on this earth is. The only *fair* in life is a carnival.

We may say, "God can do anything He wants" and generally follow it with a question as to why He doesn't do what we think is reasonable for the situation. Yes, God is sovereign and can do whatever He wants to do; however, God has limited Himself by certain things. God has granted free will (choice) to His human creation, and He will not override or overrule our choice. God will not make anyone do something against their will. God has also set into motion natural laws. An airplane that loses power in the sky will fall to earth no matter how many good people are on the inside wanting it to stay aloft.

However, it may be that one of our greatest struggles with our questions for God is that we expect Him to work on our timetable. Time is related only to this physical world. God does work within time but is not bound by it. Jesus came in *the* "fullness of time" (Galatians 4:4) which related to years of earth time, but the reality and our participation in it was conceived before time began. (1 Peter 1:20; Ephesians 1:4)

God does have His timetable and will one day set all things right. In Acts 17:30–31 Paul told his audience in Athens that although God had overlooked things done in ignorance there was going to be a day on which the world would be judged in righteousness. In Revelation 6:10 the souls under the altar asked how long God would refrain from judging and avenging what had happened to them. Much of the remainder of the Revelation deals with God indicating that He would do just that on His schedule.

One thing that seems to bring sense to some of the senselessness of life is faith. Faith gives meaning to life but does not guarantee that life will always make sense. Trusting faith in God is sometimes the only answer. God had to remind Isaiah [and us] in Isaiah 55:8–9, "'For my thoughts are not your thoughts, nor are your ways my ways,' declares the Lord. 'For as the heavens are higher than the earth, so are my ways higher than your ways and my thoughts than your thoughts.'" Therefore, we need to choose faith.

Remember, however, that even when we choose faith, struggles will still be a fact of life. Some things were set in motion before we got here. Genesis 3:17–18 says that because of Adam's sin the ground would be cursed by growing thorns and thistles and that by working the ground humanity would eat. Job 7:1 says humanity is forced to labor on earth. Job 14:1 says that a person's life is short–lived and full of turmoil. However, some struggles come because of the choices we make. Paul warns Timothy in 2 Timothy 3:12 that, "all who desire to live godly in Christ will be persecuted."

In these struggles, faith will acknowledge a divine plan that may not be seen. God, through the prophet Jeremiah, encouraged the people entering the

Babylonian captivity in Jeremiah 29:11, "I know the plans I have for you, declares the Lord, plans for welfare and not for calamity to give you a hope and a future." That plan would not unfold for another 70 years.

David in Psalm 139:16 noted that God has seen David's unformed substance and had ordained his days even before they existed. Every life is a plan of God. Holding to that belief we need to then live one day at a time trusting in His providence and power.

There is comfort in choosing faith because we know that in faith and trust we find God. When we find God, we find His peace, comfort, and strength. According to Romans 8:38–39, when we choose by faith to stay in God's care, nothing can separate us from Him. The key is putting our faith in Him realizing that sometimes God calms the storms around us and sometimes He simply calms us.

Scott Krippayne, a Christian singer, has captured these thoughts in his song "Sometimes He Calms the Storm."[22]

All who sail the sea of faith find out before too long
How quickly blue skies can grow dark and gentle winds grow strong.
Suddenly fear is like white water pounding on the soul;
Still we sail on knowing that our Lord is in control
Sometimes He calms the storm with a whispered peace be still.
He can settle any sea, but it doesn't mean He will.
Sometimes He holds us close and lets the wind and waves go wild.
Sometimes He calms the storm and other times He calms His child.
He has a reason for each trial that we pass through in life,
And, though we're shaken, we cannot be pulled apart from Christ.
No matter how the driving rain beats down on those who hold to faith
A heart of trust will always be a quiet peaceful place.

QUESTIONS

1. What are your key takeaways from these thoughts?

2. What has frustrated you the most about God ought to work in your life?

3. How difficult is it for you to wait on God even when you know He wants to bring good things into your life?

4. How do you make sense of life when it seems to make no sense?

Lesson 6

Guilt

The story is told of a little boy visiting his grandparents and given his first slingshot. He practiced in the woods but could never hit his target. As he came back to his grandparent's yard, he spied Grandma's pet duck. On an impulse he took aim and let fly. The stone hit; the duck fell dead; and the boy panicked. Desperately he hid the dead duck in the wood pile, only to look up and see his sister watching. Sally had seen it all but said nothing as she walked away.

After lunch that day, Grandma said, "Sally, let's wash the dishes." But Sally said, "Johnny told me he wanted to help in the kitchen today. Didn't you, Johnny?" As she walked by him, she whispered, "Remember the duck!" So, Johnny did the dishes.

Later Grandpa asked if the children wanted to go fishing. Grandma said, "I'm sorry, but I need Sally to help make supper." Sally smiled and said, "That's all taken care of. Johnny wants to do it." Again, she whispered, "Remember the duck." Johnny stayed while Sally went fishing. After several days of Johnny doing both his chores and Sally's, he could take it no longer. He confessed to Grandma that he'd killed the duck. "I know, Johnny," she said, giving him a hug. "I was standing at the window and saw the whole thing. Because I love you, I forgave you. I just wondered how long you would let Sally make a slave of you."

How often does guilt make us slaves? We can't enjoy life, because of the weight we carry. Guilt is like the red warning light on the dashboard of the car. You can either stop and deal with the trouble or disconnect the light.

Guilt is another of those words we use often but may never have really thought about what it means. The dictionary definition of guilt[23] is having committed a breach of conduct, especially violating a law and involving a penalty; a feeling of culpability (meriting condemnation or blame) for offenses. Another idea is that guilt is a feeling of responsibility or remorse for some offense, failure, mistake, crime or wrong, whether real or imagined. Generally, it is associated with negative feelings such as shame, remorse, anguish, torment, self–condemnation, not forgiving ourselves and self–judgment. Someone has said that guilt is the anger we turn inward against ourselves when we violate our sense of right and wrong.

When thinking about guilt in these ways, most of us easily call to mind the biblical examples of Adam and Eve (Genesis 3:1–8), David (2 Samuel 12:1–13 and his subsequent Psalm 51), Judas (Matthew 27:3–5), and Peter (Mark 14:66–72). We can see it operating as we see their behaviors. What may be less obvious is seeing it in ourselves.

Guilt may not always show itself in ways like seen in the passages above. Those who deal with its effects on us such as Kendra Cherry, a psychosocial rehabilitation specialist, psychology educator, and author of the *Everything Psychology Book,* have pointed out it may also be seen in nervousness, depression, defensiveness, suspicion of others, sleeplessness, fear, panic attacks, escapism, insecurity, being extremely judgmental, lack of concentration, shallow friendships, blaming others, self-contempt, putting oneself down, self-condemnation, addictions or other destructive behaviors and a works or performance-based lifestyle.[24] It is true these behaviors may indicate other causes, but we should not dismiss guilt as one of those causes.

It is good to be able to recognize guilt, but there is an even more important decision regarding guilt. Is it genuine or imagined? Genuine guilt is when a person is truly in violation of a standard of right and wrong. In the case of a believer, it is a violation of God's standard revealed through His word. Imagined guilt is a feeling of guilt without having committed any violation. For instance, In the Prison Fellowship newsletter, Jubilee, Charles Colson told of a young boy who became excessively fearful during the great New York blackout of 1977. When his parents questioned their son, he confessed that at the exact moment the lights went out, he had kicked a power line pole because he was mad at something. As darkness engulfed the city, he thought he was to blame and would be punished.[25] That is an imagined guilt.

Another question, in light of an apparent attitude of trying to do away with guilt might be, "Can guilt be a good thing?" A logical answer would be, "Yes"; when it leads a person to change a wrong behavior or to correct destructive thinking. Going back to Peter, although he had been warned of his upcoming actions, he denied it strongly affirming his undying loyalty. (Mark 14:29–31) Knowing that he did it, we see his remorse as he went off to weep bitterly. Luke 22:62) In the passage in Luke, we may overlook something else Jesus said to Peter. Luke 22:32 records that Jesus, in this conversation about Peter's upcoming denial, said, "When once you have turned again, strengthen your brothers." Peter's guilt apparently led him to take a hard, honest look at himself. Following Jesus' appearance to Peter and the others after His resurrection, Peter's actions were different. They were actions of faithful service as he led and strengthened the other apostles and the early Christians.

In 1 Corinthians 5, a man who took his father's wife and the attitude toward that sin by the Corinthians, were sternly rebuked by Paul. That reprimand worked and brought about a remorse that changed their actions and thoughts as well as the man who sinned. As Paul writes his second letter to the Corinthian Christians, he acknowledged the sorrow he caused. However, he then said that sorrow needed to turn to forgiveness so that fellowship and harmony could be restored instead of overwhelming guilt. (2 Corinthians 2:6–7) This kind of guilty "sorrow" brings a person to repentance which produces "repentance without regret leading to salvation." (2 Corinthians 7:9–10)

Guilt works when a person's conscience is touched by the recognition of having violated the standard of right and wrong. But is conscience alone a good indicator of guilt? To that we must say, "No." Paul tells Timothy in 1 Timothy 4:1–2 that many will fall away from the faith [here meaning that which is right] because they will have been led astray by liars whose consciences are seared [hardened; unable to feel guilt] as with a branding iron. There are those who seemingly do not have the ability to be touched with remorse or guilt. Others, like Paul himself, have consciences that recognize their sins and are led to correct them.

H. C. Trumbull once said that conscience tells us that we ought to do right, but it does not tell us what right is.[26] Journalist Sidney J. Harris remarked that once we assuage our conscience by calling something a necessary evil, it begins to look more and more necessary and less and less evil.[27] Another sage has said, "The trouble with the advice 'Follow your conscience' is that many people follow it like a person follows a wheelbarrow—they direct it where they want it to go and then follow behind."[28] It may simply be that some people won't listen to their conscience because they were told not to take the advice of strangers.

Our problem, however, is not to keep from feeling guilty but to overcome the guilt we carry. Again, there is no shortage of advice from those around us. It may be that the majority of those you would seek might simply say, "Give yourself permission to be human. After all, we all make mistakes." Others might suggest letting it go. The past is past so let it alone. Don't go asking for trouble or making yourself feel badly about what has happened. As Dr. Phil might ask, "How's that working for you?"

May I suggest that one key factor in overcoming guilt is to honestly determine whether it is genuine or imagined. One facet of this topic is the fact that some people face what is called *survivors guilt*. This guilt begins as a question as to why one person is not directly affected by some event and another person is. The person who did not suffer an injury or whatever the event brought about, may then feel guilty that others did. It may be likened to two police officers responding to a call in which one is shot and killed. The surviving partner may then carry guilty feelings as if they were responsible to the suffering of the fallen officer's family although the real guilt lies with the perpetrator of the crime. In this case, the surviving officer continually accuses himself of not doing enough to keep the death of the other officer from happening.

As Christians, we need to realize that when we begin to accuse ourselves through this kind of imagined guilt, we have a supporting cast. Revelation 12:10 says that Satan is the "accuser of the brethren." He will fuel our fires of guilt, causing us to feel so guilty that we will convince ourselves God could not possibly forgive us, much less love us.

At this point we must turn to God's word just as we do to overcome doubt. Yes, Romans 3:23 says that, "all have sinned." We know that all too well and feel remorse and guilt. We also know Romans 6:23 says that, "the wages of sin is death"; again we are aware of that consequence. But don't stop reading at the comma, semicolon, or whatever mark of punctuation your version uses. That verse continues by saying that, the "free gift of God is eternal life in Christ Jesus." We do not have to carry that guilt.

1 John 1:9 says. "If we confess our sins, he is faithful and righteous to forgive us our sins and to cleanse us from all unrighteousness." As we are baptized into the death of Christ our old self of sin is buried and we are raised to walk in a newness of life, freed from sin and its guilt. (Romans 6:4–7) Therefore we can confidently say with Paul in Romans 8:1, "Therefore, there is now no condemnation to those who are in Christ Jesus."

In the song, "You are More" by 10th Avenue North,[29] I think we find a great truth to help us finding the wind beneath our wings as we shed our guilt. It is the truth of 2 Corinthians 5:17, "If anyone is in Christ, he is a new creature; the old things passed away; behold new things have come."

There's a girl in the corner

With tear stains on her eyes
From the places she's wandered
And the shame she can't hide.
She says, "How did I get here?
I'm not who I once was.
And I'm crippled by the fear
That I've fallen too far to love.
But don't you know who you are,
What's been done for you?
Yeah don't you know who you are?
You are more than the choices that you've made,
You are more than the sum of your past mistakes,
You are more than the problems you create,
You've been remade.
Well she tries to believe it
That she's been given new life
But she can't shake the feeling
That it's not true tonight.
She knows all the answers
And she's rehearsed all the lines
And so she'll try to do better
But then she's too weak to try.
But don't you know who you are?
You are more than the choices that you've made,
You are more than the sum of your past mistakes,
You are more than the problems you create,
You've been remade.
'Cause this is not about what you've done,
But what's been done for you.
This is not about where you've been,
But where your brokenness brings you to.
This is not about what you feel,
But what He felt to forgive you,
And what He felt to make you loved.
You are more than the choices that you've made,
You are more than the sum of your past mistakes,
You are more than the problems you create,
You've been remade.
You've been remade. You've been remade.
You've been remade. You've been remade.

QUESTIONS

1. What are your key takeaways from these thoughts?

2. Why do you think it is so easy for guilt to become our taskmaster?

3. What do you consider a key question about guilt?

4. How should we use the guilt we carry?

Lesson 7

Fear

Many of us are aware of common fears. For instance: *Hydrophobia* is the fear of water [rabid animals will not drink]; *claustrophobia* is the fear of confined spaces and *triskaidekaphobia* is the fear of the number "13." See if you can match up some of these other fears.[30, 31]

_____ Levophobia   A. fear of objects on the left side of the body

_____ Dextrophobia   B. fear of objects on the right side of the body

_____ Auroraphobia   C. fear of the northern lights

_____ Calyprophobia   D. fear of obscure meanings

_____ Phobophobia   E. fear of being afraid

All of us have experienced the feeling of fear, but would we be able to define it? According to the dictionary, fear is a feeling of anxiety and agitation caused by the presence or nearness of danger.[32] Have you ever noticed how the teasers for upcoming news reports seem geared toward making us anxious about something? Have you also noticed that the emotion of fear is aroused by *potential* danger? There are legitimate events and situations that elicit fear. There are also many perceived events and situations which can bring fearful feelings, yet never happen. The feeling may still be as intense with real danger as with perceived danger.

I am sure that most of us remember our biology classes when we learned about the *Fight or Flight syndrome* that kicks in when fear is aroused preparing us for whatever action is deemed appropriate. Without too much imagination, it is easy to recall the rapid heart rate, tightening muscles, sharpened or redirected senses and increased sweating that may accompany the feeling of fear. We may not be aware that blood pressure increases. If we were to observe another person feeling fear, we would notice the dilation of their pupils to allow more light to enter the eye for vision. These are classic physical signs of fear.

What is not so obvious is the spiritual symptom of fear. Fear on the spiritual level may not produce such noticeable signs as those listed above, but I believe it is one of the more powerful variables for taking the wind from beneath our wings and causing us not to soar or live to the heights we desire. Simply stated the spiritual symptom of fear is bondage. Paul stated it this way in Romans 8:15, "For you have not received a spirit of slavery leading to fear again."

Fear may be the catalyst that is responsible for doubt, unbelief, and hopelessness.

Is there an antidote to fear, an opposing force that will overcome it? If you were asked this question, how would you respond? Probably the answer given most often would be courage. Sometimes courage is simply doing what is needed even when you are afraid. May I suggest to you the opposite of fear is *love*? John said, "There is no fear in love; perfect love casts out fear." (1 John 4:18)

The number of human fears is extensive and continues to grow. It appears that for everything on earth there can be a corresponding fear. As mentioned earlier, there are only two in-born fears in a person—the fear of loud noises and falling. All other fears are learned fears that we add to ourselves.

As discussed in a previous chapter, we fear loss in all its forms, even emotional loss. We fear the loss of our property, security, dreams, and love. It seems what we fear could be summed up in what we are experiencing—life. We fear losing so we hold back, in order that when we lose it, we will not have lost much. Related to that, it may be our biggest fear is simply death, and so we do not live full lives. In Hebrews 2:14–15, the writer talks about how because of the fear of death we were subject to slavery all our lives. Lori Ballen has used the word fear as an acronym: False Evidence Appearing Real.[33] In these verses from Hebrews, it seems that Satan has the power of death. I would ask you, however, to notice the other thoughts of those verses. Jesus became human to free us from that power.

Jesus tells His disciples in John 16:33 that the things He spoke to them were so they would have peace. He told them there would be tribulation in the world, but they should have courage because He had overcome the world. He overcame all this world threw at Him including death. It is His resurrection that gives us the truth and hope to hold on to in moving through this fear. Paul states in Romans 6:9, 11, "Knowing that Christ, having been raised from the dead is never to die again; death is no longer master over him … even so consider yourselves … alive to God in Christ Jesus."

I am also convinced that most of what we fear, both physically and spiritually, relates to one concept—inadequacy. We fear coming up short, or not making it, and thus we don't do much, so we won't have failed at much. This may explain why public speaking is generally rated among our top fears.

It may be that our preachers have helped us learn this by often quoting Romans 3:23, "All have sinned and fall short of the glory of God." This is not said in a critical way because it is the truth as revealed by God and experienced by us all. I do, however, fault those who stop reading or quoting the Bible too soon. Although Scripture says we fall short, the next verse, Romans 3:24 says that we are justified as a gift through His grace. Our inadequacy is filled because of God's mercy. Through Him who knew no sin, but was made sin on our behalf, we are able to stand before God in His righteousness, just as if we had no sin [the meaning of justification].

Still, we feel fear on occasion. To overcome fear, some therapists encourage their clients to face their fears, gradually putting themselves deeper and deeper into situations designed to help them feel more at ease and powerful in challenging those feelings of fear. Let's do that in an imagined scenario. Suppose you were called into your boss's office and told, "Everyone ahead of you in the company is gone. You are now the leader. It is now your job to carry this company forward on the new project." How would you feel? What would you do?

That may never happen to you, but it did happen to one man. In Joshua 1:1–5, God came to Joshua and told him Moses was dead and it was now his job to take the people of Israel into the Promised Land. How do you think Joshua felt?

You must remember that Joshua had been with Moses since they had left Egypt having witnessed the plagues and the parting of the Red Sea. He had stood at the base of Mount Sinai when Moses received the Ten Commandments. He had been one of the 12 spies who had scouted the Promised Land 40 years earlier. I am sure he remembered the battles they had fought along the way and knew there would be more ahead. He also knew how fickle these people could be and how they could and would complain about the smallest thing.

Perhaps that is why God encouraged him and gave him a prescription for overcoming any fear he might have. In Joshua 1:6–9, God told Joshua,

> Be strong and courageous, for you shall give this people possession of the land which I swore to their fathers to give them. Only be strong and very courageous; be careful to do according to all the law which Moses my servant commanded you; do not turn from it to the right or to the left, so that you may have success wherever you go. This book of the law shall not depart from your mouth, but you shall meditate on it day and night, so that you may be careful to do according to all that is written in it; for then you will make your way prosperous, and then you will have success. Have I not commanded you? Be strong and courageous! Do not tremble or be dismayed, for the Lord your God is with you wherever you go.

Notice the three points God makes. First, study and meditate on God's word. Paul would agree with this idea as he exhorts Timothy to, "be diligent to present yourself approved to God as a workman who does not need to be ashamed accurately handling the word of truth." (2 Timothy 2:15) Second, God says to do what you read and learn. John encouraged his readers that, "whoever keeps his word, in him the love of God has truly been perfected." (1 John 2:5) Of course we all remember James' teaching to be, "doers of the word and not merely hearers who delude themselves." (James 1:22) Finally, God simply says, "Trust Me!"

I am reminded of a man who had been employed on a building project and assigned to a night crew. Busy on the edge of a wall several stories above the ground, he suddenly lost his balance and fell but managed to grasp the edge of the wall with his fingers. Desperately he held on, hoping that his plight would be discovered. Shouting into the darkness below the level of the wall, his cries were lost in the chatter of the riveting machines, the puffing of hoisting engines, and the other sounds arising from such a project. Soon he felt his arms grow numb, and his fingers begin to slip, even against every effort of his will to hold them rigid. Frantically he tried to pray, but no miracle occurred. At last, his fingers slipped from the wall, and, with a retching sob of sheer terror, he fell—about three inches to a scaffold that had been there in the darkness all the time!

I believe I know some people like that. Thinking their salvation depends on their endurance, and conscious of their weakness, they are fearful, anxious, and unhappy most of the time: yet underneath them, all the while, are the everlasting arms of a faithful, loving, and all–powerful God who loves them.

To overcome our fear, we must learn to reverence and trust God. Even great Bible characters have had to learn and live this lesson. In Exodus 14:13, standing at the shore of the Red Sea, Moses tells the people, "Do not fear! Stand by and see the salvation of the Lord which he will accomplish for you today." Before God gave His prescription to Joshua, Moses had told him, "The Lord is the one who goes ahead of you; He will be with you. Do not fear or be afraid." (Deuteronomy 31:8) David left this thought with Solomon, "Be strong and courageous and act; do not fear nor be dismayed for the Lord God my God is with you. He will not fail you nor forsake you." (1 Chronicles 28:20) The Hebrew writer encourages us in Hebrews 13:5 by saying, "for he himself has said, 'I will never desert you, nor will I ever forsake you.'"

One of my favorite Old Testament stories related to this is from 2 Chronicles 20:1–25. The situation: the sons of Moab and Ammon and some of the Meunites had come to make war against Jehoshaphat. Jehoshaphat calls the people together to pray for God's deliverance since, "we do not know what to do." (v. 12) During the assembly, a Levite by the name of Jahaziel stood up and said, "Do not fear or be dismayed because of this great multitude, for the battle is not yours but God's." (v. 15) According to God's direction the people of Judah arrived at the wilderness of Tekoa. Jehoshaphat counseled the people, "Put your trust in the Lord your God and you will be established. Put your trust in his prophets and succeed." (v.15) The implication regarding the prophets is not just trust in them, but in the words of God they speak. The next action is most interesting.

Jehoshaphat placed a chorus of Levites ahead of his troops to lead the army into battle. I feel sure this did not have the same effect as Scottish bagpipers reportedly had against their enemies.[34] These Jewish singers went ahead of the army singing praises; "Give thanks to the Lord, for His lovingkindness is everlasting" to be exact. (v. 21) When that happens, the rest is history. God caused the Moabites, Ammonites and Meunites to fight among themselves and destroy each other. Indeed, the battle had been the Lord's as Israel never fired a shot.

It may not be that God will miraculously wipe out everything you fear. What He will do is give you the backup you need. Do you remember the story of Elisha's servant waking up in Dothan to the sight of Aram's army surrounding the city? His question to Elisha is the same question we ask when we feel surrounded, "What shall we do?" (2 Kings 6:15) Elisha calmly replies to him as God's promises do to us, "Do not fear, for those who are with us are more than those who are with them." (v. 16) When God opened the eyes of the servant, he saw horses and chariots surrounding the besieging army. (v. 17)

I am also reminded of a time shortly after David became king. The Philistines came against Israel and, after inquiring of God, David went out and defeated the Philistines. However, as they often did, the Philistines returned. This time God had David not attack them head on. His instructions were,

You shall not go directly up; circle around behind them and come at them in front of the balsam trees. It shall be, when you hear the sound of marching in the tops of the balsam trees, then you shall act promptly, for then the Lord will have gone out before you to strike the army of the Philistines. (2 Samuel 5:23–24, also 1 Chronicles 14:14–15)

Again, God gave the victory to David.

It may not be that God will give you visible or audible signs of His presence. The key may be in asking, "Do I believe He is with me and helping me?" The answer to that question is a resounding, "Yes!" "I am the Lord your God who upholds your right had, who says to you, 'Do not fear, I will help you.'" (Isaiah 41:13)

During the 1980 Winter Olympics in Lake Placid, New York, the American hockey team was made up of men barely out of their teens, some in college, some just out of college, but all untested amateurs. Most of the sports writers and others gave them no chance to win anything because, somewhere in the rotation, they would have to face a powerful, almost invincible Russian team that no American team had beaten for 20 years.

Surprisingly the Americans won their first three games moving them into a medal round. In this semi–final game they came face to face with the Russians. In the locker room before the game, coach Herb Brooks looked into the faces of his players and among his comments said, "Men, you were born to be hockey players, every one of you. And you were meant to be here tonight. This is your time."[35] Following his speech, the team rose in unison and skated onto the ice and into history as they defeated the Russians and Finland to win the gold medal.

As Christians, we have been born for courage and victory. We have been created in the image of God and crowned with glory and honor. (Genesis 1:26–27; Psalm 8:5) God encouraged Israel by saying, "Do not fear for I have redeemed you; I have called you by name; you are Mine!" (Isaiah 43:1) He encourages us and gives us the wind beneath our wings through the words of Paul in Romans 8:31–37, where He expressly says, "If God if for us, who is against us?" (v. 31); "Who will separate us from the love of Christ? Will tribulation, or distress, or persecution, or famine, or nakedness, or peril or sword?" (v. 35) [The implied answer is "No."]; and "in all these things we overwhelmingly conquer through Him who loved us." (v. 37)

QUESTIONS

1. What are your key takeaways from these thoughts?

2. What is your first reaction when you are afraid?

3. How have you let fear shut down your life?

4. What fears has God helped you overcome?

Lesson 8

The Masquerade Ball:
Denial & Isolation

I am certain you are aware these lessons have not always gone in a straight line. Much of what we have talked about, in psychological terms, is the pathology of spiritual healing—the things that are causing the trouble. I know there are folks that do not experience some of the things we have talked about—at least to the extent that I have outlined in some of these lessons. However, this lesson may strike closer to home than many are willing to admit.

In Matthew 6:16–18 Jesus said,

> Whenever you fast, do not put on a gloomy face as the hypocrites do, for they neglect their appearance so that they will be noticed by men when they are fasting. Truly I say to you, they have their reward in full. But you, when you fast, anoint your head and wash your face so that your fasting will not be noticed by men, but by your Father who is in secret; and your Father who sees what is done in secret will reward you.

Aside from its obvious implications about fasting, do you think this applies to Christians today? If so, how should it be lived out or what would a person practicing the gist of these verses look like? Perhaps you have taken the gist of these words to justify hiding your problems and struggles from others. If you have, you might have found the result producing denial and isolation which then blocks the spiritual healing you seek.

Denial, as they say, is more than a large river in Africa. Bev Smallwood defined it as "a rejection of external reality that feels too threatening. Unconsciously, semi-consciously or consciously, you refuse to perceive disturbing facts in order to ward off the anxiety they stimulate."[36] This denial comes not only because of the death of someone you know, a divorce or any number of other losses; it may also come from a perceived hurt or action toward you.

Denial for some folks gives them a case of "Scarlett Fever." This is not the acute contagious febrile disease caused by a hemolytic streptococcus and characterized by inflammation of the nose, throat and mouth…and a red rash.[37] This is the kind of fever for which Scarlett O'Hara is known; the kind that says, "I won't think of it now … I'll go crazy … I'll think of it tomorrow."[38]

Others might be described as ostriches with their heads in the sand. An interesting observation from Pliny the elder (23–79 AD) who wrote that ostriches "imagine when they have thrust their head and neck into a bush, that the whole of their body is concealed."[39] Actually, that's a myth. Ostriches do not bury their heads in the sand. When an ostrich senses danger and cannot run away, it flops to the ground and remains still, with its head and neck flat on the ground in front of it. Because the head and neck are lightly colored, they blend in with the color of the soil. From a distance, it just looks like the ostrich has buried its head in the sand because only the body is visible. However, I digress.

Denial is a psychological defense for us, an emotional circuit breaker helping us in times of severe distress.[40] [The appendix at the end of this book may help you determine if you are in denial.] Denial becomes harmful when it causes us *not* to acknowledge:

1. The facts before us. We may hear or see something but convince ourselves it is not true. Later we may say, "Why didn't I see that?" In actuality, you did, but you denied it and would not acknowledge it.

2. The practical significance of what it means. Although we may see how it affects others, we discount or deny its effect on us.

3. The emotional impact on us. We attempt to intellectualize the emotion or fear the emotion will be too strong for us. Our stock response when anyone asks us about it is, "I'm fine, really." [Have you recognized yourself yet?]

The problems denial may cause us include cutting off the information we may need for problem–solving since we refuse to acknowledge either the problem or its causes. We become defensive and hurry to change the subject of conversation when things begin to get too close.

Denial may also cause us to turn to what John James and Russell Friedman call STERBs—Short-Term Energy-Relieving Behaviors.[41] To escape the pain of the emotion we may be feeling we may turn to food, anger, exercise, work, isolation, or other behaviors that make us feel differently but do nothing to solve the problem.

Denial, since it keeps us in our own small, unreal world, can cause us to draw back from the help and support we need—both physically and emotionally. We isolate ourselves; lock ourselves in our own prison. In 1642, Richard Lovelace spent seven weeks in Gate House, a prison in Westminster, England. While there he wrote the poem, "To Althea, From Prison." You will easily recognize these words from the last stanza: "Stone walls do not a prison make; nor iron bars a cage."[42] Many critics believe the context and meaning of those lines indicate that Lovelace did not consider his circumstance capable of restraining his love. We, on the other hand, know all too well how our thoughts can hold us captive as strongly as any walls or iron bars.

What causes us to withdraw into ourselves and away from others? Far from being an exhaustive list, may I suggest the following ideas to which you are welcome and encouraged to add your own.

1. We may think no one will understand our problem or has ever had anything like it. We convince ourselves that everyone else is doing better than we are. It may simply be that others are doing a better job of hiding it than we are. It has also been my observation that, from a Christian perspective, we all seem to be hiding away from others because of sin in our lives. Knowing the truth of Romans 3:23 that *all* have sinned, we nevertheless seem convinced we are the only ones falling into this one. We believe 1 Corinthians 10:13 that no temptation has overtaken us, but, such as is common to humankind, we do not see others fighting the same struggles. Thus, we push away those who would help. Although the situations of others may be different because of each person's individuality, this does not mean they cannot empathize or care for us. Have you never reached out to help a fellow struggler through compassion and concern only to be pushed away?

2. We may isolate ourselves because we fear an embarrassing reaction from others. We may fear the questions they may ask or the remarks they may voice. We may even fear we might respond in a way that would embarrass our self. It seems to be much easier to sit in silence that face the truth.

3. We may find it difficult to trust others because we see a resemblance in them to others who have hurt us before. Our youngest daughter

brought home a dog one day that had been abandoned near the house of her friend. Several years later, my wife took the dog to the vet for a shot. Sitting in the waiting area amid the other owners and pets, our dog suddenly bristled when a particular person walked into the room. Other indications seemed to point to possible abuse at the hands of its original owner and the underlying anger appeared whenever someone of that ethnicity got around her. We, too, can place people of a certain type into one box without differentiating individual merits.

4. We may crave so much attention and seek help so strongly that we dri0ve people away from us. As others withdraw from us, our fear is reinforced. It becomes a self–feeding cycle of reaching for help, being turned away, withdrawing to be safe but eventually reaching out again until we crash into our own internal void.

This downward spiral must be stopped. Someone must stop the merry–go-round so we can get off. That someone is you and me in our own individual circumstances.

If you realize you are in denial, one of the first things you must do is to commit to honesty. Be honest with yourself regarding the facts of whatever happened. Write them out simply but honestly. Be honest in expressing the way you feel and what you believe about the situation. Emotions are not right or wrong, they just are. We all have feelings, and we need to learn to own them honestly. The key is not simply controlling your emotions but being honest about them. Then be honest in sharing with others. This does not mean that every detail is exposed but be honest that something is bothering you and share that feeling with them in non–judgmental or accusing terms.

If your isolation has caused you to withdraw from social contact, choose to take small steps that help you open up with people in places and at times you feel comfortable. You still have the choice to accept help or not but allow yourself to at least recognize the help they offer and give serious consideration as to whether it would help. If at some point you choose to reach out, go slowly but consistently in small ways that will build trust with those beyond yourself.

It takes a lot of energy to build walls to hide behind and always put on the right face; energy that causes us to lose the wind beneath our wings. The rising current we need is believing God loves us for who we are, and so do our Christian brothers and sisters. Allow the love of God and the love of your Christian family to hold and strengthen you. David said in Psalm 46:1,

"God is our refuge and strength, a very present help in trouble." Paul wrote in Ephesians 4:32, "Be kind to one another, tender–hearted, forgiving each other, just as God in Christ also has forgiven you." Sanctus Real in their song "Forgiven,"[43] said it this way:

Well, the past is playing with my head
and failure knocks me down again
I'm reminded of the wrong that I have said and done
And that devil just won't let me forget.
In this life I know what I've been
But here in Your arms, I know what I am
I'm forgiven
I'm forgiven
And I don't have to carry the weight of who I've been
'Cause I'm forgiven.
My mistakes are running through my mind
And I relive my days in the middle of the night.
When I struggle with my pain, wrestle with my pride
Sometimes I feel alone, and I cry.
In this life, I know what I've been
But here in Your arms, I know what I am
I'm forgiven
I'm forgiven
And I don't have to carry the weight of who I've been
'Cause I'm forgiven.
When I don't fit in
And I don't feel like I belong anywhere
When I don't measure up to much in this life
Oh, I'm a treasure in the arms of Christ
'Cause I'm forgiven.
I'm forgiven
And I don't have to carry the weight of who I've been
'Cause I'm forgiven

QUESTIONS

1. What are your key takeaways from these thoughts?

2. What do you think makes denial so much like fear?

3. What part about denial creates the most pain for you?

Lesson 9

Accepting Responsibility

So far in our study we have looked at some of the things that can bring disharmony into our lives causing us problems in our relationship with God. These include doubt, fear, guilt, anger, and our misbeliefs. Generally, these are not the sole causes, but most often come as a result of some other event in our lives like a loss from a death, a job, our health or a loss of trust in someone else.

"It is as if one day you're on top of the world.[44] Everything is going well, God's in His heaven and all's well with the world." Then suddenly, the world is on top of you. What you thought was supposed to happen doesn't and the answers you have don't fit the questions being asked. What happens then?

When that happens, understand that what you are experiencing can and will change you. This is both the good news and the bad news of the situation. However, neither the amount nor intensity of the stressors in your life are the strongest indicators of future spiritual problems. The key to adjustment is what you believe about the events in your life and how you respond to it. The model illustrating this point would look like this:

Character—Comfort—Crisis *leading to* **Choice** or **Calamity**

Do you remember the lame man we discussed in lesson 2 from John 5? There, it was stated that for any healing to take place, whether physical or spiritual, one key question must be answered by the one who is affected. It is the question Jesus asked a lame man in John 5:6, "Do you wish to get well?" The power to heal is available. There is a wind blowing beneath your wings that can lift you into the sky. Unfortunately, I observe folks, including myself, who practice victimhood rather than choosing to fly.

This victimhood way of living is based upon a misbelief of *externalism*. Externalism is another way of talking about *locus of control*. Locus of control refers to the degree to which an individual feels a sense of agency in regard to his or her life. Someone with an internal locus of control will believe that the things that happen to them are greatly influenced by their own abilities, actions, or mistakes. A person with an external locus of control will tend to feel that other forces…are more responsible for the events that occur in the individual's life.[45] An external locus of control tells me that my happiness and spiritual well-being depend on the people and circumstances outside myself. Part of an old Hee-Haw skit with Archie Campell and Roy Clark and friends may illustrate this.[46]

Archie: Hey I guess you heard about my terrible misfortune.
Roy: No, what happened?
Archie: Yeah, my great uncle died.
Roy: Oh, that's bad!
Archie: No, that's good!
Roy: How's come?
Archie: Well, when he died, he left me 50,000 dollars.
Roy: Oh, that's good!
Archie: No, that's bad!
Roy: How come?
Archie: When the Internal Revenue got thru with it, all I had left was 25,000 dollars.
Roy: Oh, that's bad.
Archie: No, that's good.
Roy: How come?
Archie: Well, I bought me an airplane and learned to fly.
Roy: Well, that's good.
Archie: No, that's bad.
Roy: How come?
Archie: Well, I was flying upside down the other day, and I fell outta the dern thing.
Roy: Well, that's bad.
Archie: No, that's good.
Roy: How come?
Roy: Well, when I looked down under me and there was a great big ole haystack.
Roy: Well, that's good.

Archie: No, that's bad.

Roy: How come?

Archie: Well, I got a little closer and I saw a pitchfork aimed right at me

Roy: Well, that's bad.

Archie: No, that's good.

Roy: How come?

Archie: I missed the pitchfork.

Roy: Well, that's good.

Archie: No, that's bad.

Roy: How come?

Archie: I missed the haystack too.

Notice how the perceptions change related to the circumstance? What seems lost in all of this is the person involved in the story.

Yet, like so many other things people may practice, there are benefits of being a victim. When I say this, I am not referring to someone who has suffered trauma or injury at the hands of another person. The idea under discussion here is our attitude of being a victim. Those who have this attitude may feel:[47]

1. They are not responsible for their attitudes or actions. "You made me angry." "If you had not done_____, then I would not have had to do_____."

2. They feel sorry for themselves, but do not seem to want to find a solution to their problem. They internalize negative messages and negative self-talk.

3. There is an attitude of powerlessness that may spill over into frustration and resentment against a world that seems to be against them.

In December 2020, Dr. David Ley, in an article posted by *Psychology Today*, described people with this attitude in these words:

We all know that person. Every bad thing that happens to them. They seem self–absorbed, but in a strangely negative way. The world is out to get them. It's not paranoia, but it can seem delusional with the way they constantly interpret things as being intentional to harm and punish them. Nothing is ever really their fault, because of all the bad things that happen to them. And they aren't responsible for the bad things they do, because they've been through so much, and they are just getting some of theirs back.[48]

Interestingly, feeling like a victim may be more than a passing feeling brought on by certain circumstances. Israeli researchers Rahav Gabay, Boaz Hameiri,

Tammy Rubel-Lifschiltz, and Arie Nadler have suggested a personality construct they call the Tendency for Interpersonal Victimhood (TIV) and define it as "an enduring feeling that the self is a victim across different kinds of interpersonal relationships."[49] They wrote that this tendency for victimhood is a 'stable personality characteristic'.[50]

These researchers conducted eight studies among Jewish-Israelis and believed there are four key components contributing to this tendency. They include:

1. Need for recognition refers to the victim's motivation to have their victimhood acknowledged and empathized with.[51]

2. Moral elitism refers to the victim seeing themselves as morally pure and right while seeing others as immoral, unfair, or selfish.[52]

3. Lack of empathy refers to an oblivious reaction to others in general and to their suffering in particular. This means a preoccupation with the victim's own suffering and decreased attention and concern about others.[53]

4. Rumination refers to a focus of attention on the symptoms of the victim's distress and its possible causes and consequences rather than its possible solutions.[54]

These researchers concluded that those exhibiting TIV were "less willing to forgive others after an offense, and more likely to seek revenge rather than avoidance and behave in a revengeful manner.[55] Those with this tendency toward victimhood believed they were "entitled" to behave aggressively and selfishly because of what had happened to them.[56] Individuals exhibiting a relatively high level of TIV present themselves to others as weak victims who have been hurt and in need of protection and who feel they are considerate and conscientious people who must face a cruel and abusive world.[57] Although taken in a rather restrictive sample of people, their findings were consistent throughout the studies and tests they ran, and the researchers believe their findings are relevant to other contexts and populations.[58]

If such components and conclusions do carry over to other populations and you become a complaining, finger–pointing, poor–me person you may ensure that your problems will grow bigger in your life. You will become angrier at your lack of power. After all, as a victim you are not in control of what happens to you.

Although this sounds like, and is, a downwardly-spiraling circle which appears to lead only to more and more misery and heartache, there is a way to keep from being pulled under. A person who wants to find the wind beneath their wings again must begin to accept responsibility. At first blush, the argument might be, "How can I accept the responsibility of what is happening to me if it is not my fault?" What is happening to you may be out of your control, but it is not 100% responsible for the way you may be feeling or thinking. Your reaction to what is happening is most certainly in your control.

In his book, The 7 Habits of Highly Effective People, Stephen Covey wrote about a discovery that changed him. While on sabbatical with his family in Hawaii, he came across a book with a paragraph thought that "basically contained the simple idea that there is a gap or space between stimulus and response, and that the key to both our growth and happiness is how we use that space."[59] In other words, between when something happens to us and we react or respond to it there is a space where we can choose how we will react or respond. Between stimulus and response is our greatest power—the freedom to choose.[60]

Covey called people who allow their circumstances to determine their actions reactive.[61] In contrast, Covey proactive are those who realize they are responsible to their own lives; that behavior is a function of decisions and not conditions.; and who take the responsibility to make things happen.[62] He continued:

Look at the word responsibility—"response-ability"—the ability to choose your response. Hight proactive people recognize that responsibility. They do not blame circumstances, conditions, or conditioning for their behavior. Their behavior is a product of their own conscious choice, based on values, rather than a product of their conditions based on feelings.[63]

John James and Russell Friedman echoed the same idea when they wrote:

As children, we could not change the actions of parents and other adults. Sometimes after our childhood, we may become aware of events that happened before we had the power to alter them. We must take responsibility for our current reaction to what happened in the past. Otherwise, we will forever feel like a victim.[64]

Their solution to the dilemma of victimhood is to take 1% responsibility for your reaction. They called this 1% a small key that unlocks a large door to open your head and your heart to what needs to be done.[65] That one percent is your thoughts and reactions to whatever event has caused you to lose the zest and joy you once had. By accepting 1% of the responsibility, you are acknowledging that you have chosen to feel hurt, angry, or betrayed. That choice has caused you to act accordingly and for your mind to find justification. Yet just as there are benefits for holding on to a victim attitude, there are beneficial considerations related to accepting 1% of the responsibility of your life.

For one thing, you don't have to change everyone else around you for your life to improve. If you have chosen *how* you perceive any event in your life, that chosen perception affects everything you do and your reactions to everyone else around you. It is much like the poem by Jessie Belle Rittenhouse that goes:

> I bargained with Life for a penny,
> And Life would pay no more,
> However I begged at evening
> When I counted my scanty store;
> For Life is a just employer,
> He gives you what you ask,
> But once you have set the wages,
> Why, you must bear the task.
> I worked for a menial's hire,
> Only to learn, dismayed,
> That any wage I had asked of Life,
> Life would have paid.[66]

Paul understood the gist of those words. Remember his statement from Philippians 4:11, "I have learned to be content in whatever circumstances I am in"? Paul was no victim. Sure, bad things happened to him that were beyond his control and that colored his world. However, he decided he would choose the color. Also, Paul reminds us from Romans 8:28 that, "all things work together for good to those who love God, to those who are called according to His purpose." My choice should be to love God and not try to be in control of everything and everyone. As Paul would also reveal to us in Romans 14:12, "Each one of us will have to give an account of himself to God." I won't have to account to God for you or you for me.

Another benefit of accepting responsibility is that you do not become frustrated when the people you try to change don't. Accepting responsibility for my feelings eliminates my having to change everyone else. Reinhold Niebuhr expressed it this way in his "Serenity Prayer"[67]—'Grant me the serenity to accept what I cannot change, the courage to change what I can, and the wisdom to know the difference.' The wise man of Proverbs 3:5–8 wrote,

Trust in the Lord with all your heart and do not lean on your own understanding. In all your ways acknowledge Him and He will make your paths straight. Do not be wise in your own eyes; fear the Lord and turn away from evil. It will be healing to your body and refreshment to your bones.

Might I also suggest that when we are willing to accept 1% of the responsibility of our feelings and behaviors, we may find other folks are willing to help us with whatever problem we are facing. Instead of finding folks who are *responsible* for my problem, I will find people wanting to help me find a way through.

Imagine if you will what it must have been like in Jerusalem shortly after the day of Pentecost. Acts 2:41 says that 3,000 people responded to the preaching that day and began meeting and sharing as a church. Surely some of those people were from the list of nations Luke shares in verses 9–11. Suppose also they enjoyed this fellowship so much they decided to stay in Jerusalem instead of going home. In fact, verse 42 takes that thought out of the realm of conjecture as Luke says, "They were continually devoting themselves to the apostles' teaching and to fellowship, to the breaking of bread and to prayer."

At some point for one of these folks this joy might begin to take on a different feeling. Running short of money, perhaps with no job or definite place to stay, I wonder if this person might think, "Why did I let that man persuade me to do this? And why did these other Jews talk me into staying so long? What am I going to do now?"

I find it hard to convince myself of that scenario because I am convinced that those who became Christians on that day accepted the responsibility for what they had done. If a problem arose for them, I do not believe they would have failed to make that known to someone or that help would have not already been on its way. Luke goes on in Acts 2:44–45 by writing, "And all those who had believed were together and had all things in common; and they began selling their property and possessions and were sharing them with all, as anyone might have need."

For these benefits to bless our lives we must quit saying, "You are responsible for what's happening to me." Instead, we need to accurately answer the question, "Who is responsible for what?" Other folks may have done something that has brought unwanted things into your life; however, no matter what others do, you have the choice of how you accept it. As Joshua 24:15 says, "Choose you this day whom you will serve."

Understanding that I have a part in the overall scheme of my life also causes me to shift my focus to what I can do differently. If all I do is focus on the "what-ifs"—What if they had not done this? or What if there had only been ...?—I will always be looking in the rearview mirror of life. Things could always have been done differently or better. Things can also be done differently or better than it was before when the opportunity presents itself. This is also a choice that I must make—"that whatever your hand finds to do, do it with all your might." (Ecclesiastes 9:10)

To strengthen your resolve to find the wind beneath your wings make this commitment to accept responsibility: I choose responsibility. Though I may have been victimized, I refuse to become a victim, wallowing in self-pity. Though I may have had no control over what happened to me, I choose to exercise control over my own thoughts and actions. I realize I cannot change someone else, nor does my recovering and healing depend upon someone else changing. Therefore, I choose to look at the resources I have and the actions I can take. I identify small steps that move me along the pathway that leads to spiritual joy and blessings. I choose to see the blessings among the struggles and determine to be thankful for them.[68]

QUESTIONS

1.   What are your key takeaways from these thoughts?

2.   How do you see yourself—victim or victor?

Lesson 10

Powerlessness or Purpose

On a day that few in this generation will ever forget—September 11, 2001—Christine Pisera Naman gave birth to a son, Trevor, in Pennsylvania. Because of what she felt on that day she compiled a book of other babies born on that day.[69] Her book, *Faces of Hope,* shares pictures of one baby from each state born on that fateful day. In her dedication of the book, she wrote:

> To all of the moms who brought good people into the world
> on a day when it needed it most.
> To all the babies who had the courage to be born into the world
> on a day when the world didn't even have the time to welcome you.
> We know you will make the world a better place. Be good.
> To all the moms who gave birth to these babies
> whose fathers were lost on September 11, 2001.
> You are our heroes. We won't profess to know your pain or struggle.
> But our hearts are with you.
> We all get up on the morning for the same reason.
> We all go on because there are babies to raise.
> To all of the children who lost someone they loved on September 11, 2001.
> I'm sorry you heard words that no child should ever hear.[70]

One of the children featured in the book was Christina-Taylor Green, born to Roxanna & John Green of Maryland. That name may ring a bell with you if you also remember the shooting in Tucson, Arizona on January 8, 2011. Christina was the 9-year-old girl killed in that attack on Congresswoman Gabriella Giffords.[71]

Tom Clancy was once asked about the difference between reality and fiction. He said, "Fiction has to make sense."[72] It is a real struggle for us to make sense out of some things that happen; but we try. Unfortunately, we sometimes get stuck in trying to make sense of the senseless and stall our spiritual healing.

Before we get too much further into this particular discussion, allow me to share with you some bad news. Sometimes there are no inherent and/or good reasons for the horrible things that happen.

Some have tried to compile possible reasons for bad things happening. Sometimes a person simply makes a foolish choice that had far–reaching consequences. Sometimes a person is in the wrong place at the wrong time. For instance, in April 2007, 32 students died at the hand of a gunman at Virginia Tech who himself was also killed.[73] Those students were where they were supposed to have been, and the gunman chose their room. Sometimes there are natural laws that create bad events such as the Japanese earthquake and tsunami in March 2011.[74] The only other reason is that we are citizens of a fallen and sinful world.

Considering those reasons some folks quickly ask, "Does God cause bad things to happen?" Generally, it seems that this question has an underlying implication that the bad things that happen should be regarded as punishment from God. A short response is that God does not cause them to happen in a direct sense, although He does permit things to happen as consequences of choices and actions.

Allow me to illustrate it this way: If one of my children gets my permission to use my car but has a wreck while driving, did I cause the wreck? A reasonable person would answer "No" although I created the potential for that by allowing my car to be used. Thus, it is the ability to choose that God has given to every human being who can bring about tragedy and senselessness in this world through the choices made.

Every individual has made or will make some "bad" choices. Hopefully we learn from them and begin to make better choices. A person who continues to make "bad" choices may find themselves in a position of powerlessness because of the consequences of those choices and may find themselves with some other problem.

As discussed in the last lesson, some folks have a victim mentality. This may be a result of too many "bad" choices. They began to feel as if they have no power and that nothing will ever be taken care of. Jeremiah voiced that kind of attitude in Jeremiah 8:20–22 when he said,

Harvest is past, summer is ended, and we are not saved. For the brokenness of the daughter of my people I am broken; I mourn, dismay has taken hold of me. Is there no balm in Gilead? Is there no physician there? Why then has not the health of the daughter of my people been restored?

The story is told of a man who went to work with both ears bandaged. "What happened?" asked one of his associates. "I was ironing my shirt; the phone rang; but I accidentally picked up the iron," he replied. "Then what happened to the other ear?" *"They called back."* Some people do not learn from their mistakes. Growing up, I remember hearing the phrase "Live and Learn" being said quite often. Unfortunately, I have since observed that some people only live, they never learn.

There is also the tendency to stop taking positive action toward the accomplishment of anything in life. Becoming like a stick in a river, a person with this tendency simply goes where the current moves them with no resistance. Sometimes it is not that they take no action, they just don't take positive action. I heard a story of a man diagnosed with pancreatic cancer. The prognosis given him was 6 months. This man elected not to have any treatment. Thinking about it for a few days, he decided to stop paying on his house. He withdrew his life's savings and spent it traveling. Toward the end of the 6 months, while on a trip, he noticed he wasn't feeling badly and, in fact, had gained weight. Returning home, he went back to the doctor. His doctor said there had been a mistake. He had only had pancreatitis and not cancer, by the time the mistake had been found, no one knew how to contact him.

Although earlier in this lesson I shared with you the bad news about the things that happen to us and take the wind from beneath our wings, allow me to now share with you some good news. Sometimes there is no good or reasonable answer as to why bad things happen, but that does not mean that good things cannot come from them. For many folks, even in the darkest hour, there is a lifeline they hold to. It is Romans 8:28, "We know that God causes all things to work together for good to those who love God, to those who are called according to His purpose."

I find it interesting that when bad things happen we are quick to ask, "Why me?" I know for myself that I am hoping to understand the steps that brought this result. However, when something good and enjoyable happens to me, and I observe the same reaction, in others, I never ask, "Why me?" Maybe it's because I assume that good things are what I am supposed to receive and not bad things. I do not believe that I am as understanding as Job when he said, "Shall we indeed accept good from God and not accept adversity?" (Job 2:10)

What we need to understand is that good things come because of our choices in much the same way bad things happen because of our choices. The choice for good to come through the events of my life is to choose to love God as Romans 8:28 says. In choosing to love God, we choose purpose over powerlessness and increase the probability of finding meaning and direction for our lives.

Ben Sherwood in his book, *The Survivors Club*, lists purpose as one of the tools that should be in our "survival kit." He wrote:

> Purpose is the booster rocket of survival. It gives you the power and drive to persevere in the face of incredible adversity. You have big goals that you strive for—they're the reason you're alive, and they make every day worthwhile. You have a passion for life and your dreams. You believe that life is a gift and it's up to you to make the most of it. You're determined in the face of adversity and focused on accomplishing your objectives. You confront your challenges with unwavering conviction. You have a mission in life, a reason for living that is greater than yourself. You are driven by a profound sense of duty to a cause, whether it be God, country, family or friends. You work tirelessly and are willing to sacrifice deeply for your purpose and principles.[75]

Doesn't that sound like the life you want to live? Wouldn't that put the wind beneath your wings? Yet as good as it sounds and as much as we may desire that outcome in our lives there remains one question, "How do I choose purpose over powerlessness?" Let me suggest some answers to that question.

First, commit to aligning yourself with God's intent to bring good out of life's events. When Paul wrote to the Christians in Philippi, he shared with them some ways to do this. In Philippians 2:1–4 he told them to look beyond themselves. Specifically in verses 3–4 he said, "Do nothing from selfishness or empty conceit, but with humility of mind regard one another more important than yourselves; do not merely look out for your own personal interests, but also for the interests of others." Where would we be if God was only concerned about Himself? How small a package we make wrapped up in ourselves. In that condition, we leave little room for anyone else, including God.

Next, I see Paul telling those Christians not to sweat the small stuff. Philippians 4:6–7 says, "Be anxious for nothing, but in everything by prayer and supplication with thanksgiving let your requests be made known to God. And the peace of God, which surpasses all comprehension, will guard your hearts and your minds in Christ Jesus." Do you get the idea that everything was the small stuff to Paul? In verses 11–12 of that same chapter Paul says that he has been, and is, content in whatever circumstances in which he finds himself. He does that by turning it all over to God with thanksgiving and keeping his thoughts on the true, the honorable, the right, the pure, the lovely, the good, the excellent and the praiseworthy of life. (Philippians 4:8)

Above all, Paul says he does not allow himself to stall out or get stuck in the past. Paul did not think that just because he could be content in circumstances or think good thoughts that such was the sum total of life. Listen to his proclamation in Philippians 3:12–14:

> Not that I have obtained it or have already become perfect, but I press on that I may lay hold of that for which I also was laid hold of for Christ Jesus. Brethren, I do not regard myself as having laid hold of it yet, but one thing I do: forgetting what lies behind and reaching forward to what lies ahead, I press on toward the goal of the upward call of God in Christ Jesus.

Did you hear that? Paul did not say it was all because of his own will power. He moves forward to lay hold of that which has gotten hold of him. That is something that all Christians have. We have been grasped by God, filled with His Spirit and given a living hope, an imperishable inheritance reserved in heaven. (1 Peter 1:3–4) With that power and being surrounded by that great cloud of witnesses (Hebrews 12:1), how can we keep from straining forward? That alone should put some wind under our wings and in our sails.

However, in looking *beyond* ourselves we also need to look *at* ourselves and recognize the gifts/talents/abilities God has given us and use them. Romans 12:6 tells us we have differing gifts and we are to exercise them. 1 Peter 4:10 says we ought to use the special gift each of has received in serving one another as "good stewards of the manifold grace of God." Ephesians 4:16 says that the growth of the body (the church—Ephesians 1:22) is done when each part and each joint supplies what it has to offer.

Someone has suggested that in doing these things, what we are really doing is committing ourselves to make a difference. Paul told the Philippians (1:21–26) he was struggling with a weighty decision. He wanted to leave this world and be with Christ, but he also wanted to continue living to encourage and help the Philippians Christians in their Christian walk. Paul knew that staying would make a difference for them and so he was convinced that would remain. I believe that Paul was the inspiration for a quote a friend of mine always uses to close emails they send to me. That quote is, "Aspire to inspire before you expire!"

Victor Frankl, a survivor of several Nazi prison camps, including Auschwitz, explained how a person can endure and survive under the most difficult conditions. He said, "Everything can be taken from a man but one thing; the last of human freedoms—to choose one's attitude in any given set of circumstances, to choose one's own way."[76] Frankl wrote movingly about the importance of having an aim—or goal—in life. He wrote, "There is nothing in the world, I venture to say, that would so effectively help one to survive even the worst conditions as the knowledge that there is meaning in one's life. There is much wisdom in the words of Nietzsche: 'He who has a *why* to love for can bear almost any *how* ...'"[77]

Sometimes it is the small things that seem to trip us up taking the wind from beneath our wings as Francesca Battistelli sang in her song "This Is The Stuff." However, her message is clear: Trust God, thank Him for these things and choose to let Him use this stuff to make us who He wants us to be and to rise on the wings of eagles.

This Is the Stuff [78]
by Francesca Battistelli

I lost my keys
In the great unknown
And call me please
'Cuz I can't find my phone
Oh!
Chorus:
This is the stuff that drives me crazy
This is the stuff that's getting to me lately
In the middle of my little mess
I forget how big I'm blessed
This is the stuff that gets under my skin
But I gotta trust You know exactly what You're doing
It might not be what I would choose
But this is the stuff You use

45 in a 35
Sirens and fines
While I'm running behind
Whoa

Chorus

This is the stuff that drives me crazy
This is the stuff that's getting to me lately
In the middle of my little mess
I forget how big I'm blessed
This is the stuff that gets under my skin
But I gotta trust You know exactly what You're doing
It might not be what I would choose
But this is the stuff You use
I lost my keys in the great unknown
And call me please 'Cuz I can't find my phone
This is the stuff that drives me crazy
This is the stuff that's getting to me lately
In the middle of my little mess
I forget how big I'm blessed
This is the stuff that gets under my skin
But I gotta trust You know exactly what You're doing
It might not be what I would choose
But this is the stuff You use
Forthy-five in a thirty-five
Sirens and fines while I'm running behind
Whoa
This is the stuff that drives me crazy
This is the stuff that's getting to me lately
In the middle of my little mess
I forget how big I'm blessed
This is the stuff that gets under my skin
But I gotta trust You know exactly what You're doing
It might not be what I would choose
But this is the stuff You use
So break me of impatience
Conquer my frustrations
I've got a new appreciation
It's not the end of the world
Oh Oh Oh
This is the stuff that drives me crazy
This is the stuff
Someone save me
In the middle of my little mess
I forget how big I'm blessed

This is the stuff that gets under my skin
And I've gotta trust You know exactly what You're doing
It might not be what I would choose
But this is the stuff You use
Oh Oh Oh Oh
This is the stuff You use

QUESTIONS

1. What are your key takeaways from these thoughts?

2. God created you and has a plan for your life. What do you think that plan is?

Lesson 11

Healing Within the Body

Dwight L. Moody told the story of a young boy who began attending a Sunday school in his neighborhood. When the boy's parents moved to another part of the city the little fellow still attended the same Sunday school, although it meant a long, tiresome walk each way. A friend asked him why he went so far, pointing out there were plenty of other Sunday Schools just as good nearer to his house. "They may be as good for others, but not for me," was his reply. He was then asked, "Why not?" "Because they love a fellow over there," he replied.[79] If only we could make the world believe that we loved them there would be fewer empty churches, and a smaller proportion of our population who never darken a church door. Let love replace duty in our church relations, and the world will soon be evangelized.

Although these lessons on spiritual healing are primarily directed toward each of us as individuals, I want to throw in another angle to consider as we seek to find God's wind beneath our wings. Although much of our healing will come through a rethinking and renewal of our relationship with God, that healing can be helped or hindered by those around us.

The church has been criticized for being the only army that shoots its own wounded. By wounded, I mean those who have been wounded by sin. Because the expectations of living a holy and blameless life are so high, because the standard of being a Christian are above those of worldly living, many times in the church, it's difficult to find forgiveness, and, in some cases, depending upon the nature of the sin, we do not grant persons the grace to begin a fresh start with the record wiped clean.

I am sure you remember Pat Tillman. Pat Tillman played safety for the Arizona Cardinals of the National Football League. In 2001 he walked away from a $3.6 million dollar contract to join the Army following the terrorist attack of September 11, 2001. He became an Army Ranger and was deployed to Afghanistan. He was killed in action on April 22, 2004 and posthumously awarded the Silver Star for Combat Valor and the Purple Heart for being wounded in combat. The initial report of the incident said he was killed by enemy fire as he charged the enemy following a mortar attack allowing his platoon to escape. However, a subsequent investigation and report indicated that a land mine explosion was mistakenly perceived to be a mortar attack and another group of Army Rangers seeing four Afghan fighters in Tillman's group mistook them for the enemy and fired on them killing Tillman and one of the Afghan men as well as wounding three other American soldiers.[80]

In combat, such occurrences involve what is called "friendly fire". Friendly fire is defined as inadvertent firing towards one's own or otherwise friendly forces while attempting to engage enemy forces, particularly where this results in injury or death.[81] It is not:

1. A death resulting from a negligent discharge
2. Murder, whether premeditated or in the heat of the moment
3. Deliberate firing on one's own troops for disciplinary reasons

Some folks might even consider such things to be the "collateral damage" of warfare. Collateral damage is defined as damage that is unintended or incidental to the intended outcome.[82]

No matter how it may be considered, the danger of things like this happening is within the realm of possibility for the church. Listen to Paul's warning to the churches of Galatia in Galatians 5:13–15:

> For you were called to freedom, brethren; only do not turn your freedom into an opportunity for the flesh, but through love serve one another. For the whole Law is fulfilled in one word, in the statement, you shall love your neighbor as yourself. But if you bite and devour one another, take care that you are not consumed by one another.

Although there are many ways by which we may "pull the trigger" of friendly fire within a congregation, allow me to simply share one which seems to be a major part of our societal fabric—competition. The spirit of competition was evident among the apostles as Mark points out in Mark 9:33–34, "They came to Capernaum; and when He was in the house; He began to question them, 'What were you discussing on the way?' But they kept silent, for on the way they had discussed with one another which of them was the greatest." It even appeared in the early church. Note 3 John 9, "I wrote something to the church; but Diotrephes, who loves to be the first among them, does not accept what we have to say."

We may be so conditioned to competition we do not see the potential dangers it fosters. One of those is judgmentalism. We may become like the Pharisee of Luke 18 as he prayed in verse 11, "Thank You that I am not like other people: swindlers, unjust, adulterers, or even like this tax collector." Who became the standard for his comparison? Wasn't it himself? Thus, he wanted God's mercy withheld from the publican. From whom do you withhold mercy?

Another danger is insensitivity. We do not seem to have much regard for weaklings; for those who can't "cut it". It has been my observation that sometimes those who are not *keeping up* with whoever the leader is or with whatever attitude is prevailing are often left behind. The story is told of a small-town drunk who saw the preacher on the street and said, "Some boys from your church threw rocks at me last night." "Maybe they were trying to make a better man out of you," the preacher replied. "But preacher, I never heard of Jesus throwing rocks at people to make them better."

How many times have we perhaps been like the Pharisees who criticized Jesus when He ate with the tax collectors and sinners in Matthew's house? (Matthew 9:9–11) Or like the crowd gathered that day ready to throw stones at the woman taken in adultery? (John 8:1–11) In both instances Jesus stood against their critical attitude as he said, "It is not those who are healthy who need a physician, but those who are sick. But go and learn what this means: 'I desire compassion and not sacrifice,' for I did not come to call the righteous but sinners." (Matthew 9:12–13) When no one was left to condemn the woman, neither did Jesus.

Henri Nouwen, a Catholic priest, wrote a book entitled *The Wounded Healer*.[83] His basic theme was that each of us is wounded in some way by society, and all of us are wounded by sin. His thesis is that in our woundedness, if we choose to remain alone, we do not really become healed. If we do not internalize our woundedness but reach out to others in sharing and compassion to their hurts, we find healing. Although Nouwen is not always fully orthodox in some of his stated beliefs, I believe his picture captures the essence of the healing we can find within the body of Christ.

Again, the key question asks, "How do I become a wounded healer?"

I am convinced a vital answer to that question is, "Forgive others." By inspiration Paul reinforces this answer in the following passages:

Ephesians 4:32—"be kind to one another, tender-hearted, forgiving each other, just as God in Christ also has forgiven you."

Colossians 3:12–13—"So, as those who have been chosen of God, holy and beloved, put on a heart of compassion, kindness, humility, gentleness and patience; bearing with one another, and forgiving each other, whosoever has a complaint against anyone; just as the Lord forgave you, so also should you." [By the way, the word used here for *complaint* means to blame[84] which we sometimes are too quick to do when we don't get our way.]

Following the prayer Jesus gave to His disciples in Matthew 6:9–13, He adds this warning in v. 14–15: "For if you forgive others for their transgressions, your heavenly Father will also forgive you. But if you do not forgive others, then your Father will not forgive your transgression." Can it really mean that the forgiveness I desire from God is dependent upon my willingness to forgive others?

I am sure you recall Peter's question of Jesus in Matthew 18:21 about how many times he should forgive anyone who sins against him. Peter simply voiced the question we each carry silently at times. Since you remember the question, I am sure you also remember the answer Jesus gave him—not seven, but seventy times seven. If that answer was not sufficient, Jesus added the parable of the unforgiving servant who was forgiven a massive debt but refused to forgive an insignificant debt owed him. That action cost the unforgiving servant dearly as his debt was renewed but now, he was in prison and unable to repay.

Just like the warning following Jesus' prayer in Matthew 6, I wonder if sometimes we overlook verse 35 in this parable when He says, "My heavenly Father will also do the same to you, if each of you does not forgive his brother from his heart"? That raises the bar from just saying the words but still holding a grudge to being fully sincere with the forgiveness I offer.

Another answer is to encourage those who stumble. The exhortation of 1 Thessalonians 5:14 is to, "admonish the unruly; encourage the fainthearted, help the weak, be patient with everyone." There is indeed a time to admonish the unruly as 1 Corinthians 5:1–7 would show. Unruly folks are those who show a continual attitude of rebellion and contentiousness, but a good chewing out is not in order for someone who has momentary lapse of virtue. The Hebrew writer adds this, "Therefore strengthen the hands that are weak and the knees that are feeble, and make straight paths for your feet, so that the limb which is lame may not be put out of joint, but rather be healed." (Hebrews 12:12–13) In the context of our own body, we help any wounded member so that the injury does not become worse or spread. The same holds true for the spiritual body of believers.

We cannot overlook the many "one another" passages of the New Testament teaching us how we should behave and feel toward other Christians.

Romans 12:10—"devoted to one another in brotherly love"

Romans 12:16—"be of same mind, not haughty in mind, associate with lowly

Romans 13:8—"love one another" (John 13:34–35; 1 Peter 1:22; 4:8; 1 John 3:11, 23; 4:7, 11)

Romans 14:13—"do not judge one another"

Romans 14:19—"pursue things that make for peace" (1 Thessalonians 5:13)

Romans 15:7—"accept one another"

Romans 15:14—"admonish one another"

1 Corinthians 12:25—"same care for one another" [Does not mean we have the same relationship with one another, but we help one another,]

Galatians 5:13—"serve one another" (1 Peter 4:10)

Galatians 5:26—"do not envy one another"

Ephesians 4:32—"kind, tender–hearted, forgiving one another"

1 Thessalonians 5:11—"encourage one another" (Hebrews 3:13)

Hebrews 10:24—"stir one another up to love and good works"

James 4:11—"do not speak against one another"

A lone eagle may look majestic soaring in the sky, but we are not alone. The church is a group of people so we are more like geese who fly in formation so that we can help each other. The "V"– shape formation in which geese fly reduces the air drag (air resistance) that each bird experiences when in flight in comparison to a bird flying solo. This allows them to cover longer distance with much less effort. For example, geese can achieve a greater distance of about 70 percent when flying in groups than each flying solo, using the same amount of energy.[85]

There are other benefits of flying in this "V" position. Every bird in the group fly in the field of vision of all other members. This helps in keeping track of each other in the group. This also makes it conducive to the members in the group to communicate with each other while in flight. For example, if one bird should become sick or has been injured by some means such as being shot, then, that bird will fall out of formation. This will then result in two other geese falling out with the wounded goose to help and offer protection and will remain until that bird recovers or dies before rejoining the other geese. It is important to note also that military jets fly in this V formation for the same reasons. Each fighter pilot can see, communicate, and help each other while in flight, working as a team.

John Donne wrote the famous refrain, "No man is an island entire of itself; every man is a piece of the continent, a part of the main."[86] Paul said, "For not one of us lives for himself, and not one dies for himself." (Romans 14:7) As Christians, we are members one of another.

We Are the Body [87]
By Casting Crowns

It's crowded in worship today
As she slips in
Trying to fade into the faces.
The girls' teasing laughter
Is carrying farther than they know
Farther than they know
But if we are the body
Why aren't His arms reaching?
Why aren't His hands healing?
Why aren't His words teaching?
And if we are the body
Why aren't His feet going
Why is His love not showing them
There is a way, there is a way.
A traveler is far away from home.
He sheds his coat
And quietly sinks into the back row.
The weight of their judgmental glances
Tells him that his chances are better out on the road.
But if we are the body
Why aren't His arms reaching?
Why aren't His hands healing?
Why aren't His words teaching?
And if we are the body
Why aren't His feet going
Why is His love not showing them there is a way
Jesus paid much too high a price

For us to pick and choose who should come
And we are the Body of Christ.
If we are the body
Why aren't His arms reaching?
Why aren't His hands healing?
Why aren't His words teaching?
And if we are the body
Why aren't His feet going
Why is His love not showing them there is a way?
Jesus is the way.

QUESTION

1. What are your key takeaways from these thoughts?

Lesson 12

The Best Question[88]

During the Vietnam War, communist guerrillas were constantly on the move through the jungles. They were unable to confine their prisoners in a compound, so they constructed small cages made of bamboo as cells. These cages averaged about 5 feet in length and about 4 feet wide and high, much too small for an average American to stretch out or be comfortable.[89] Some POWs were kept in these "tiger cages" for up to six years. One Navy flier reported that one night he was able to work one of the bamboo sticks loose and step outside the cage. Just those few moments of freedom helped him forget his current condition. It is terrible when human beings imprison other human beings against their will. More tragic is when an individual does it to himself or herself by self–defeating thoughts and actions.

As we have noted throughout this study, our most asked question is "Why?" I think we ask this because we believe there are practical and rational answers for everything. We also believe we should be able to find those answers if we just look hard enough. The crowning achievement to that search will be that upon finding the answer, everything will make sense.

Pardon my skepticism, but I sometimes wonder if we ask this question simply to regain the control we thought we had over life. We are convinced we could find "closure" if enough questions are answered. It may be that we are seeking to rewrite the ending or that we simply want to protect ourselves and others in the future.

There are, however, some problems related to a determined search for the final why. One is that we fall prey to what has been called analysis paralysis.[90] We search and question things repeatedly without ever finding what we believe is the answer. During that continual searching, relationships may deteriorate as the energy needed to maintain those relationships is channeled to the search. In the end, we become more frustrated because the puzzle pieces are not falling into place. In our frustration, we lock ourselves up and throw away the key. Although there is room between the bars of our cell to walk through, we hold on one side to the past and on the other, the future unwilling to let go of the past and afraid the future will be the same as the past. Thus, we don't move.

Instead of asking "Why?", perhaps the better question is "How?". How can I effectively deal with the adversity I am facing instead of drowning in it? How can I learn what I need to know to get through this? What choices can I make to adapt to the realities of where I am and allow God to move me beyond this?

How is a better question than *why* because it is easier to answer. *Why* may not be known or something of which we are unaware. *How* traces the steps that have led us to where we are. *How* moves one to action because it doesn't require finding the meaning of life. It zeros in on one step and not the whole plan, answering the age–old question of how to eat an elephant—one bite at a time. *How* reduces anxiety by moving us to action thereby releasing the energy created by the fight/flight syndrome.

We choose to ask *HOW* by:

1. Listing the *whys* we keep asking hoping to find answers

2. Changing the *"What if"* to *"What is"*

3. Asking *how* questions

    *   How did this happen? [List each step.]

    *   How can I identify the resources I have to help me deal with this?

    *   How can I use the resources I have to help me deal with this?

    *   How can I take what I am learning and how I am growing to help others? (2 Corinthians 1:3–4)

4. Think about action and the future

Use the following passages to encourage and challenge you to action.

1. Proverbs 3:5–8—"Trust in the Lord with all your heart and do not lean on your own understanding. In all your ways acknowledge Him and He will make your paths straight. Do not be wise in your own eyes; fear the Lord and turn away from evil. It will be healing to your body and refreshment to your bones."

2. Jeremiah 29:11—"For I know the plans I have for you, declares the Lord, plans for welfare and not for calamity to give you a future and a hope."

3. Psalm 118:24—"This is the day which the Lord has made; let us rejoice and be glad in it"

4. Philippians 4:4–8—"Rejoice in the Lord always; again I will say, rejoice! Let your gentle spirit be known to all men. The Lord is near. Be anxious for nothing, but in everything by prayer and supplication let your requests be made known to God. And the peace of God, which surpasses all comprehension will guard your hearts and minds in Christ Jesus. Finally, brethren, whatever is true, whatever is honorable, whatever is lovely, whatever is of good repute, if there is any excellence and if anything worthy of praise, dwell on these things."

5. Isaiah 40:31—"Those who wait for the Lord will gain new strength; they will mount up with wings like eagles, they will run and not get tired, they will walk and not faint."

Helen Keller once said, "When one door of happiness closes, another opens; but often we look so long at the closed door that we do not see the one which had opened for us."[91] Finding the wind beneath our wings is about keeping our eyes and hearts open to the doors God is opening for us and trusting Him for the good He will bring into our lives.

QUESTIONS

1. What are your key takeaways from these thoughts?

2. What prisons might you have created for yourself?

3. What steps can you take to free yourself?

4. Do you want to free yourself?

Lesson 13

Getting Out of the Nest

Josephine Kuntz' husband was a textile worker and house painter. During the winter of 1940 he was unemployed because of a seasonal layoff and the weather. Money was not to be had. To finish the picture, their 18–month–old daughter, Rachel, was recovering from pneumonia and was not doing well. The doctor insisted Rachel eat a hard–boiled egg every day. Even that was beyond the Kuntz' reach.

One of Rachel's friends at church said they should pray for the eggs. Although a church–going family, this was not something they had ever done, but desperate times call for desperate measures. Josephine got on her knees one morning and prayed, asking God to provide the eggs her daughter needed.

According to her story as published in the book *Snowflakes in September*,[92] Mrs. Kuntz was busy in the kitchen later that morning when she heard cackling coming from her front yard. There by the fence sat a large red hen she had never seen before. The hen laid an egg, got up and went on down the road. The same thing happened the next day and continued to happen for almost two weeks. During that time Rachel's health improved, the weather improved, and Josephine's husband returned to work. The day after her husband returned to work, the hen quit coming. What can anyone do under those circumstances except thank God? God takes care of His people.

It may not always be seen in such dramatic ways, but the Bible promises that God will and does care for His own. Toward the end of Moses' life and the wilderness wanderings of Israel, Moses gave the people a song to remind them of what God had done for them. In Deuteronomy 32:9–11, we find these words,

> For the LORD's portion is his people; Jacob is the allotment of his inheritance. he found him in a desert land, and in the howling waste

of a wilderness; he encircled him, he cared for him, he guarded him as the pupil of his eye. Like an eagle that stirs up its nest, that hovers over its young, he spread his wings and caught them, he carried them on his pinions.

Verse 11 particularly fits the scope of these lessons.

This study's introduction began with the picture of an eagle soaring on the currents of the wind. We, as human beings and especially as Christians, desire to soar above the troubles of life. However, life sometimes seems to hold us earthbound. The intention of this study has been to discover those things that will give us the wind beneath our wings to reach the heights and live the life for which we have been designed by our Creator. Using the illustration of an eagle, let's apply some of the lessons we see in this magnificent bird to see how God also helps us.

An adult eagle, when the young eaglets are ready to go out on their own, will push off and hover above the nest flapping its wings to demonstrate the mechanics of flying and encourage the young birds to imitate the flapping motion. In the same way, God has demonstrated to us Himself and His love for us.

Romans 5:8—"God demonstrates His own love toward us in that which we were yet sinners, Christ died for us."

1 Timothy 1:16—"for this reason I found mercy so that in me as the foremost, Jesus Christ might demonstrate His perfect patience as an example for those who would believe in Him for eternal life."

John 1:14—"And the Word became flesh, and dwelt among us, and we saw His glory, glory as of the only begotten from the Father, full of grace and truth."

Matthew 1:23—"Behold, the virgin shall be with child and shall bear a Son, and they shall call His name Immanuel, which translated means, God with us."

John 14:7, 9—"if you had known Me, you would have known My Father also; from now on you know Him and have seen Him. ... If you have seen Me, you have seen the Father."

If the young birds flap their wings, but do not seem to want to leave the comfort of the nest, the adult bird will then begin to tear up the nest making it uncomfortable for them. How often do our lives get *uncomfortable*? As we have noticed, this is sometimes due to our choices and the consequences of those choices. However, to follow God, to accept the call and calling He places on our lives also creates some discomfort. Ask Abraham, when called to sacrifice his son, Isaac. (Genesis 22) Ask Moses, when called upon to lead Israel from Egyptian captivity. (Exodus 3) Ask Jesus, as He prayed in the Garden of Gethsemane. (Matthew 26:36–42; Luke 22:44) I fear too many of us, including myself, want to stay in our comfort zones rather than risk flying even though it is what we may desire.

Eventually, the young birds will perch on the edge of the nest and step off. Although they may spread their wings and try to fly, they are inexperienced and may begin to plummet downward. At that point, the adult bird with wings outstretched will swoop beneath the young bird catching it on its back, fly higher, releasing the young bird to try again. Does not God also watch over and deliver His people? Israel's history is replete with examples. Paul reminded Timothy about how he knew of Paul's conduct, purpose, faith, perseverance in 2 Timothy 3. Apparently, Timothy was also aware of the persecutions and sufferings Paul had experienced on his first missionary journey, particularly at Antioch of Pisidia (Acts 13:14–50), Iconium (Acts 14:1–5), and Lystra (Acts 14:8–19). However, Paul's confident assertion to Timothy in 2 Timothy 3:11 was "out of them all the Lord rescued me!" That matches the truth of Psalm 34:19, "many are the afflictions of the righteous, but the Lord delivers him out of them all."

What can we learn from this?

> We need to recognize that although there may be danger in leaving the nest, eagles are meant to fly and not sit in the nest. In the same way, Christians are meant to grow. Peter says in 1 Peter 2:2, "like newborn babies long for the pure milk of the word so that by it you may grow in respect to salvation." Paul writes in Ephesians 2:10, "for we are His workmanship created in Christ Jesus for good works which God prepared beforehand that we would walk in them."

Just as there comes a time in the life of each young eagle where they must decide to jump from the edge of the nest, there also comes a time in each person's life where a decision has to be made. For some, that may be the decision to become a Christian—to follow Christ. For a Christian, it may be the decision to go all in and trust Christ with their lives, following the Spirit's leading, and coming to know the fullness of life as they live out the will of God in their life. James challenges his readers in James 4:17, "to one who knows the right thing to do and does not do it, to him it is sin." There can be no sitting on the fence. A refusal to change is a decision; not the one God wants a Christian to make, but a decision, nonetheless.

That decision and its consequences must be made by each individual themselves. An adult eagle can teach its young, but it cannot fly for them. God, through the Spirit and His word, can teach us, but He cannot live our lives for us. It is not enough to know, we must act. That is the importance of the passage in James 4:17. It was also the conviction of Jesus in Matthew 7:24–27,

> Therefore everyone who hears these words of mine and *acts upon them* [emphasis mine], may be compared to a wise man who built his house on the rock. And the rain fell, and the floods came, and the winds blew and slammed against that house; and yet it did not fall, for it had been founded on the rock. Everyone who hears these words of mine and *does not act on them* [emphasis mine], will be like a foolish man who build his house on the sand. The rain fell, and the floods came, and the winds blew against that house; and it fell—and great was its fall.

Are you seeking to find the wind beneath your wings to soar above parts of your life? Is God trying to teach you to fly? God wants to be that wind through His Son Jesus, and the power of His Spirit in your life bringing joy, purpose, and fulfillment. You can ignore Him or resist Him, but life will go on. Will you cooperate with Him and know His blessing?

QUESTIONS

1. What are your key takeaways from these thoughts?

2. How have you seen God working to show you how to live?

3. Why do you think obedience is the deciding factor in bringing God's blessings into a person's life?

APPENDIX

From Lesson 8

Are you in denial?[93]

Maybe you've already recognized that you've been living too far from reality, or maybe you're still not sure. Your first action step will be to assess where you are right now by taking the following "Denial Quiz." Please use this scale to rate yourself on the statements that follow, indicating how true each is of you.

1—Very untrue of me

2—Untrue of me

3—Neutral

4—True of me

5—Very true of me

_____ 1. I believe I'm doing much better emotionally than others seem to think I am.

_____ 2. I've been able to stay strong, never, or rarely showing my pain.

_____ 3. I try to stay busy so that I don't have time to think about what happened to me.

_____ 4. I find myself getting emotional at strange times, overreacting or secretly fighting tears about something that doesn't even relate to me.

_____ 5. Comparing myself to others who have been through tragic experiences, I think I'm doing quite well.

_____ 6. I keep doing the same things over and over to make my life better. Though I haven't seen the results I want, I believe if I only keep doing them long enough, things will change.

_____ 7. When something upsetting happens to me, I tell myself that it really doesn't matter to me.

_____ 8. I've always prided myself on my ability to keep excellent control of my emotions.

_____ 9. Since experiencing the trauma, I've been much more easily irritated, and I often take it out on people who don't deserve it.

_____ 10. Others have tried to convince me to get help, but I know I don't need it. I can handle this myself.

Subtotal: _____ (Add the numbers you placed in the blanks above)

TOTAL: _____ (Multiply the subtotal by 2)

Interpretation: While there are some other possible explanations for a high score on a given item, a pattern of "true" or "very true" responses strongly suggests that you may be relying heavily on denial to cope and temporarily alleviate your pain. If you are past two or three months from a life–altering event, there is a strong probability that higher scores indicate an unhealthy use of denial.

Use these general interpretive guidelines to give you an idea about where you are right now.

85–100—This is an "alarming" score. If you continue your course of running from reality, you will be highly likely to compound your problems and make your recovery much lengthier and more complex.

60–84—A score in this range is "high." This suggests that you are in a danger zone; you are probably using denial in a way that could impede your progress.

45–59—If you fall within this range, you are about "average" in your use of denial as a coping mechanism.

30–44—A score falling in this "low" range suggests that you are dealing appropriately with the facts of your situation as well as acknowledging your emotional realities.

20–29—A score in this range could mean you're totally facing reality, or it could mean you're in denial. You might want to have a trusted friend or relative respond to the quiz on your behalf and compare your responses.t

Endnotes

1   William Wilson, *Wilson's Old Testament Word Studies* (McLean, VA : MacDonald Publishing Company, 1975), p. 406.

2   Joseph Henry Thayer, *Greek-English Lexicon of the New Testament* (Grand Rapids: Zondervan Publishing House, 1976), p. 677.

3   William Wilson, *Wilson's Old Testament Word Studies* (McLean, VA: MacDonald Publishing House, 1975), p. 411.

4   Thayer, p. 520–523.

5   Although there is definitive source of this quote given by Carl Sandburg, many sites attribute it to him such as https://www.goodreads.com/quotes/328746–there–is–an–eagle–in–me–that–wants–to–soar.

6   Gail Sheehy, *New Passages* (New York: Random House, 1995), p. 12.

7   The fear of falling has been deduced from a 1960's experiment by Eleanor J. Gibson and Richard D. Walk known as the Visual Cliff Experiment. The fear of loud noises was deduced from an experiment by John B. Watson and his associate Rosalie Rayner in the 1920s called the Little Albert Experiment.

8   https//history.info/on–this–day/1873–levi–strauss–receives–a–patent–for–jeans/

9   According to *Quote Investigator* (https://quoteinvestigator.com/2013/07/13/chains–of–habit/), Warren Buffet said this during a speech at the University of Florida. The quote is also attributed to Samuel Johnson and Bertrand Russell according to this website. However, Warren Buffet seems to have used it quite often.

10   There are several variations of this story. However, Roger E. Olson who authored a biography of Barth shares his research about this incident in an article found online at https//www.patheos.com/blogs/rogereolson/2013/01/ did–karl–barth–really–say–jesus–loves–me–this–i–know/.

11   This is a part of his aphorism 8 from the "Maxims and Arrows" section of his book Twilight of the Idols published in 1888.

12   φορτίον (fortion), Joseph Henry Thayer, *Greek–English Lexicon of the New Testament* (Grand Rapids: Zondervan Publishing House, 1976, p. 657.

13   Βάρη (barā), Thayer, p. 95.

14 https:// peanuts.fandom.com/wiki/December_1965_comic_strips.

15 *Webster's New World Collegiate Dictionary,* Third Edition, Victoria Neufeldt, editor in chief (New York: Macmillan, 1997), p. 410.

16 διακρίνω (diakrinō) comes from the words "dia" (through) & "krino" (to separate), Thayer, p. 138–139, 132, and 360–361.

17 Kent Crockett, *The 911 Handbook* (Peabody, MA: Hendrickson Publishers, 2003), p. 16.

18 Whether this exact quote or similar thoughts have been attributed to Seneca, Thomas Jefferson, James Garfield, Mark Twain, and others. https// quoteinvestigator.com/2013/10/04/never-happened/

19 Andrew Sinclair, *Prohibition: The Era of Excess* (Boston: Little, Brown and Company, 1962), p. 252.

20 William Wilson, *Wilson's Old Testament Word Studies* (McLean, VA: MacDonald Publishing Co.), p. 441.

21 Joseph Henry Thayer, *Greek–English Lexicon of the New Testament* (Grand Rapids: Zondervan Publishing House, 1976), p. 198.

22 "Sometimes He Calms the Storm" written by Kevin Stokes, Tony W. Wood. Published by BMG Songs/Careers BMG Music/Universal Music— Brentwood Benson Publishing/Universal Music—Brentwood Benson Songs. Recorded by Scott Krippayne in 2003.

23 Webster's New World Dictionary, Third Edition, Victoria Neufeldt, editor (New York: Macmillan, 1997, 1996, 1994, 1991, 1988), p. 600.

24 Kendra Cherry, "What is a Guilt Complex?" online at https//www. verywellmind.com/guilt–complex–definition–symptoms–traits–causes– treatment–5115946 .

25 A sermon illustration submitted to Sermon Central by David Huss, online at http//www.sermoncentral.com/sermon–illustrations/17079/in– the–prison–fellowship–newsletter–jubilee–by–davon–huss.

26 Henry Clay Trumbull quoted in the Precept Austin article "Conscience" of 1/14/2020, online at https//www.preceptaustin.org/conscience.

27 Sidney J. Harris quote found online at http//www.overallmotivation. com/quotes/sydney–j–harris–quotes/.

28 This quote by an unknown source is found online at http//bible.org/ illustration/wheelbarrow#:~:text=Like%20a%20Wheelbarrow%20The%20 trouble%20with%20the%20advice%2C,want%20it%20to%20go%2C%20 and%20then%20follow%20behind.

29 "You are More" written by Jason Ingram and Mike Donehey, recorded by 10th Avenue North, and released May 10,2010 on the album "The Light Meets the Dark".

30 Taken from a list of fears found online at https:// www.verywellmind. com/list–of–phobias–2795453.

31 In case you have trouble with this, the answers are in the same order as the fears.

32 Webster's New World Dictionary, Third Edition, Victoria Neufeldt, editor (New York: Macmillan, 1997, 1996, 1994, 1991, 1988), p. 495.

33 Lori Ballen, "F.E.A.R: False Evidence Appearing Real" online at https// loriballen.com/f–e–a–r/.

34 Following the Jacobite Rebellion of 1745, the Scottish clans used bagpipes in battle to raise moral and intimidate the opposing army according to https// picturesinhistory.com/bagpipes–an–unusual–weapon–in–the– world–wars.

35 Source unknown, found at https// wildchildsports.com/miracle– hockey–speech–with–miracle–speech–text/

36 Bev Smallwood, This Wasn't Supposed to Happen to Me (Nashville: Thomas Nelson, 2007), p. 19.

37 Webster's Seventh New Collegiate Dictionary (Springfiled, MA: G.&C. Merriam Company, Publishers, 1969), p. 769.

38 Margaret Mitchell, Gone with the Wind (New York: Scribner, 1936), p. 1036.

39 Pliny, Natural History with an English translation in ten volumes, Volume III (Cambridge, MA: Harvard University Press, 1967), p. 293. Found online at https// archive.org/details/naturalhistory03plinuoft/ page/292/ mode/2up?view=theater

40 "Denial" an online article at https// www.psychologytoday.com/us/ basics/denial.

41 John W. James and Russell Friedman, The Grief Recovery Handbook: 20th Anniversary Expanded Edition (New York: Collins Living, 2009) p. 77–81.

42 Richard Lovelace, "To Althea, From Prison" online at https// poets.org/ poem/althea–prison.

43 "Forgiven" written by Chris Robman, Dan Gartley, Matt Hammit, Peter Prevost; produced by Christopher Stevens; released on the album "Pieces of a Real Hear", released 2009.

44 These are probably the most famous and well-known lines from Robert Browning's poem, Pippa Passes, Part 1: Morning, online at https// internetpoem.com/robert-browning/pippa-passes-part-i-morning-poem/.

45 "Locus of Control" and online article found at https//www. psychologytoday.com/us/basics/locus-control.

46 Archie Campbell and Roy Clark, script for "That's Good That's Bad" routine, online at https//www.answers.com/music-and-radio/Script_ copy_of_Archie_Campbell%27s_That%27s_Good_ That%27s_Bad_ routine. The video can be seen on Youtube at https:// www.youtube.com/ watch?v=7fMnQAvz0ek.

47 Crystal Raypole, "How to Identify and Deal with a Victim Mentality" online at https//www.healthline.com/health/victim-mentality.

48 David J. Ley, Ph.D., "The Victim Personality" found online at https:// www.psychologytoday.com/us/blog/ women-who-stray/202012/the-victim-personality.

49 The information in this and the next 3 paragraphs are taken from Rahav Gabay, Boaz Hameiri, Tammy Rubel-Lifschiltz, and Arie Nadler, "The Tendency for Interpersonal Victimhood: The Personality Construct and its Consequences" pg 2. Found online at https:// www.researchgate.net/ publication/ 341548585_The_Tendency_for_ Interpersonal_Victimhood_ The_Personality_Construct_and_its_ Consequences.

50 Ibid, pg 26.

51 Ibid, p 3.

52 Ibid, p 4.

53 Ibid, p 4.

54 Ibid, p 5.

55 Ibid, p 27.

56 Ibid, p 4

57 Ibid, p 30.

58 Ibid, p 30.

59 Stephen Covey, The 7 Habits of Highly Effective People (New York: Simon & Schuster, 1989, 2004) p. 320–321.

60 Covey, p. 78.

61 Covey, p. 79.

62 Covey, p. 78.

63 Covey, p. 78.

64 John W. James and Russell Friedman, The Grief Recovery Handbook: 20th Anniversary Expanded Edition (New York: Collins Living, 2009) p. 65.

65 John James and Russell Friedman, p. 65–66.

66 Jessie Belle Rittenhouse, "My Wage" found online at https//www. greatestpoems.com/poet/jessie–belle–rittenhouse/.

67 Reinhold Niebuhr, "Serenity Prayer" found online at https// proactive12steps.com/serenity–prayer/.

68 Adapted from Bev Smallwood, This Wasn't Supposed To Happen To Me (Nashville: Thomas Nelson, 2007), p. 71.

69 Karen MacPherson, "Mother counters 9/11 tragedy with 'Faces of Hope'", Philadelphia Post–Gazette, Philadelphia, PA, September 11, 2002. Newspaper article found online at https// old.post–gazette.com/ books/20020911hope0911fnp3.asp.

70 Christine Pisera Naman, Faces of Hope (Deerfield Beach, FL: Health Communications, Inc., 2002), p. xi.

71 Emily Friedman, "Mother of Christina–Taylor Green, Shot at Tucson Event, Says Daughter Wanted to Go Into Politics", ABC news story, January 9, 2001, online at https//abcnews.go.com/US/christina–green–shot–gabrielle–giffords–tuscon–event–loved/story?id=12576408.

72 Arthur Gutch, "Tom Clancy's Top 5 Rules for Writing", October 19, 2017, online at https// blog.opyrus.com/tom–clancys–top–5–rules–for–writing#:~:text=The%20difference%20between%20real%20life%20and%20fiction%20is, have%20to%20hang%20together%20in%20a%20logical%20progression.

73 Christine Hauser and Anahad O'Conner, "Virginia Tech Shooting Leaves 33 Dead", New York Times, April 16, 2007, online at https// www.nytimes.com/2007/04/16/us/16cnd–shooting.html.

74 "Japan Earthquake: Tsunami hits north–east", BBC news story, March 11, 2011, online at https// www.bbc.com/news/world–asia–pacific–12709598.

75   Ben Sherwood, *The Survivors Club* (New York: Grand Central Publishing, 2009), p. 319.

76   Victor Frankl, *Man's Search for Meaning* (New York: Washington Square Books, 1984), p. 86.

77   Ibid., p. 126.

78   Tom Wood, Ian Eskelin & Francesca Battistelli, "This is The Stuff", released March 12, 2013, online at https//genius.com/Francesca–battistelli–this–is–the–stuff–lyrics.

79   Dwight L. Moody, "They Love a Fellow There!", *Moody's Stories* (#137868), Bible Truths online at https//bibletruthpublishers.com/they-love–a–fellow–there/dwight–lyman–moody/moodys–stories/dwight–l–moody/la137868.

80   Biography.com editors, "Pat Tillman Biography" (A&E; Television Networks: Biography.com website, April 2, 2014, updated September 12, 2022) online at https:// www.biography.com/athletes/pat–tillman.

81   https//www.merriam–webster.com/dictionary/friendly%20fire.

82   Ibid.

83   Henri J. M. Nouwen, The Wounded Healer (New York: Doubleday, 1972).

84   Henry George Liddell and Robert Scott, A Greek–English Lexicon (Oxford, England: University Press, 1940) p. 1143.

85   From a question by William Brandsmeier answered by Jeff Scott on Aerospaceweb.org on July 17, 2005 found online at https//aerospaceweb.org/question/nature/q0237.shtml.

86   "No man is an island" is a phrase that comes from a poem by John Donne entitled "Meditation XVII. It was published in 1624. Found online at https//genius.com/John–donne–meditation–xvii–annotated.

87   Mark Hall, "We Are The Body", recorded by Casting Crowns, produced by Mark Miller and Steven Curtis Chapman, released on July 26, 2003 by Beach Street Records, Nashville, TN.

88   Many thoughts in this lesson come from Bev Smallwood, *This Wasn't Supposed to Happen to Me* (Nashville: Thomas Nelson, 1978), p. 73–99.

89   Brad Lendon, "One of these Vietnam War POWs spent 10 months in a 'tiger cage.' What happened to the other was even worse", WRAL-NEWS, Raleigh, NC from The CNN Wire™ & © 2023 Cable News Network, Inc., a Warner Bros. Discovery Company. All rights reserved. Found online

at https//www.wral.com/story/one–of–these–vietnam–war–pows–
spent–10–months–in–a–tiger–cage–what–happened–to–the–other–was–
even–worse/20885355/.

90 Jodi Clarke, "What Is Analysis Paralysis?" published April 22, 2022 by
Verywellmind online at https//www.verywellmind.com/what–is–analysis–
paralysis–5223790.

91   Helen Keller, *We Bereaved* (New York: Leslie Fulenwider, Inc., 1929),
p.23.

92 Josephine M. Kuntz, "The Little Red Hen," *Snowflakes in September*
(Nashville: Dimensions for Living, 1992), pp 29–30.

93   Taken from *Smallwood,* p. 33–36.